Amazing Cake Pops

Amazing Cake Pops

85 Advanced Designs to Delight Friends and Family

Noel Muniz

Skyhorse Publishing

Skyhorse Publishing books may be purchased in bulk at special discounts for sales promotion, corporate gifts, fund-raising, or educational purposes. Special editions can also be created to specifications. For details, contact the Special Sales Department, Skyhorse Publishing, 307 West 36th Street, 11th Floor, New York, NY 10018 or info@skyhorsepublishing.com.

Skyhorse® and Skyhorse Publishing® are registered trademarks of Skyhorse Publishing, Inc.®, a Delaware corporation.

www.skyhorsepublishing.com

10 9 8 7 6 5 4 3 2 1

Library of Congress Cataloging-in-Publication Data is available on file.

ISBN: 978-1-62636-567-4

Printed in China

For my grandmother, Luz Pantoja.

*Further dedicated to all the wonderful people who have supported
The Cake Poppery over the years. This book is especially for you.*

Contents

Introduction

I was first introduced to cake pops in the fall of 2009 by my brother's fiancée. It had been several months since I left culinary school, and with student loan debt hanging over my head, I turned to catering for friends and family to help pay off my loans. My brother's fiancée was throwing a jewelry party and approached me with the idea of making ladybug cake pops for her event along with a few other items. I had never heard of the concept of cake pops at the time—they were a new twist on cake that was

barely beginning to take off. Even though I had no idea what they were and had never made them, I gladly agreed to help.

This was well before any books on cake pops were out, and very little was written on how to make them. I remember searching for cake pops on the Internet and only seeing a handful of pictures and a couple of blog posts. I didn't find anything that really explained in detail how to make them, but I was still confident I could. I figured it wouldn't be that hard to dip cake into melted chocolate. Boy, was I wrong.

The day of the event came and nothing went right. My cake and frosting mixture was far too creamy, even though I followed the directions and used the three-quarters of a jar of canned frosting the recipe called for. The dough mixture turned out too sweet and was also too creamy—it had the consistency of raw cookie dough. My chocolate ended up melting thick, like peanut butter. I couldn't keep the pops on the sticks and was about to give up.

After what felt like an eternity, I figured out how to thin down the chocolate and improvised by making truffles instead. They turned out to be some sorry-looking ladybugs by the time I was done, but I had finished, and that is all that mattered. They were not the prettiest, neatest, or best-tasting pops, but everyone at the party seemed to love them and asked where they could purchase them.

As the months passed, requests for baked goods slowly started to pour in. I was cooking less and baking more. Although I had attended culinary school, I had very little experience with baking—I left well before the topic of baking was ever covered. The only experience I had with baking at the time was from boxed cake mixes and premade cookie dough. So I had no choice but to start learning how to bake properly. With each order, my baking skills improved, and I learned more techniques. Slowly but surely people kept coming to me for cake pops and cake balls. I started off selling mainly cake balls for friends and family. I would only make a few every now and then as I continued to work on improving my skills. Eventually, I noticed a huge demand for the sweet treats.

At the time, there were only a handful of bakeries across the United States selling cake pops and cake balls. Most of them focused only on cake balls, and no one focused on making completely customizable cake pops. My experience with cake pops was still highly limited, and I was far from mastering the art, but I decided I would start the first custom cake pop shop and call it "The Cake Poppery." I was going to become a cake pop artist—not just any cake pop artist, one of the top artists in the field.

From then on, I focused on growing my business and achieving my goal. I concentrated on one order at a time, and each one brought new and exciting challenges. Everything I know about cake pops was learned through trial and error. I quickly figured out what worked and what didn't, and what the best ways were to market and sell them, especially since many people had not heard of them at the time. It wasn't easy at first—mistakes were made and lessons were learned.

Running a cake pop business might seem like a wonderful and relaxing business to be in, but it's not. It is very draining and stressful, especially when you first start out and have never run a business or had experience working in one. You spend hours sitting in front of a computer answering emails; your hands, back, and neck start to hurt from all the rolling and decorating; things always find a way to go badly and you become emotionally drained; you lose money well before you start to pull a profit; you get scammed and taken advantage of by people. You need thick skin to deal with difficult customers who try to belittle you, but in the end, it's all worth it. You are not just making pops, you are making memories. You get to meet some of the most amazing people, and they allow you to be a part of some of the most important events and occasions in their life. They come to you for their wedding order, which leads to a baby shower and a first birthday. You get to see kids grow up before your eyes, and you are able to put a smile on their faces..

Had you asked me what I was envisioning for my future while I was still in culinary school, baking would have been the very last thing to come to mind. I would have never imagined that years later I would be baking professionally; that I would have made thousands of cake pops and shipped them all over the United States. I would be stunned to know that I would end up writing a book on cake pops— a topic I knew absolutely nothing about and have come to love. I would never trade this experience for anything else in the world.

This book is my way of saying thank you to all the wonderful customers and fans that supported me all these years. It is my gift to you—this is the only way I can show my appreciation as I pass on everything I have learned over the years about the art of cake pops to a new set of cake pop artist all over the globe. I hope this book inspires you.

Getting Started

Fundamental Cake Pop Supplies

A cake pop artist is only as good as the tools he or she owns. Making cake pops does not require many tools, but there are certain items that are necessary. Plenty of fantastic designs can be made with the bare minimum, but with the help of a few specialty baking items, ordinary pops can be turned into extraordinary works of art. There are so many useful items sold in stores that can help you become a better artist. Never limit yourself to just the baking supply aisles in craft stores—you can find many molds and cutters in the jewelry and clay sections, too. Here are some of the most important and versatile tools to help take your pops to the next level.

Stand mixer

Although a stand mixer is not necessary, it makes binding the cake with the frosting a breeze. You can mix your cake with frosting by hand, but it is messy and more time consuming. Using a stand mixer is a clean and fast method that perfectly blends the two together without leaving behind any large chunks of cake.

Digital scale

A digital scale is your best friend when making cake pops. It allows you to make sure all your pops are the same exact size and weight. By hand weighing the pops on a digital scale, you are able to produce much more consistent results. The ideal weight for a cake pop is one ounce of cake filling; it is the perfect serving size and surface area for decorating.

Cookie scoops

Cookie scoops are a great alternative to digital scales. They come in a wide variety of sizes and can quickly separate large amounts of cake uniformly without you having to hand weigh the cake.

Lollipop sticks

Lollipop sticks are a must-have item when making cake pops. They come in a wide variety of sizes and types. You can use paper, plastic, or wooden sticks, as well as paper straws. Plastic sticks come in a variety of colors and are great to use if you have issues with paper sticks turning yellow from absorbing fat. The ideal stick is six inches long, as it gives you plenty of room to hold the pop comfortably while decorating, and it looks nice when displayed in a stand.

Cake pop stands

A durable stand is essential when making cake pops in order to keep the pop sturdy and upright while it dries. You can buy one at most craft stores, and it can be made from wood, paper, plastic, or metal. You can also use Styrofoam to hold your cake pops, but the foam will flake off and get messy. Another issue with using Styrofoam is the holes created from the sticks will become loose over time with repeated use and won't be sturdy.

Cookie cutters

Cookie cutters are wonderful tools to utilize. They come in all sorts of sizes and designs and can be used in various ways. The small-sized cookie cutters allow you to create shapes that would have been otherwise impossible. Using them as a mold allows you to create pops with sharper edges and in obscure shapes that are not achievable through hand sculpting. The ideal size cutters to use are two inches or smaller; anything larger and the pops will be too heavy to dip. Look for nesting cookie cutter sets typically meant for fondant, as those are the perfect size to use as a mold.

Floral gum paste cutter sets

A floral gum paste set can be used for making flowers and other accents. A small rose petal cutter can be used for creating the ear of a mouse or the wing of a bird. Larger petals can create bunny ears, or a daisy can become a collar for clown pops.

Molds

Whether they are chocolate or fondant molds, these are great to have on hand to add little details to cake pops. They are perfect to utilize when you want to add small details like bows, flowers, buttons, or seashells without the use of fondant. Using a mold is a quick way to create accent pops that take little effort and time.

Pasta machine

A pasta machine is great to use when rolling out fondant. It allows you to roll the fondant to the same thickness and ensure uniformity when working with large amounts. It also ensures everything dries at the same rate. Use it on the thinnest setting to make paper-thin fondant for the skirts or ruffles of dress cake pops.

Paintbrushes

Every cake pop artist should have at least two sets of paintbrushes in various widths and sizes. Stiff- and soft-bristle sets are a must-have. The stiff-bristle paintbrushes come in handy when making textures like fur, grass, or wood grains, as well as adding textured flowers using the brush embroidery technique. You want to use the soft brushes when adding or using luster or petal dust, as well as when painting details onto the pops. With a soft-bristle brush you can add rosy cheeks to babies and add highlights to different shapes. An airbrushed effect can also be achieved with a soft-bristled paintbrush and petal dust.

Plastic bags

Plastic bags make wonderful piping bags for adding small details to cake pops. Fill them with chocolate and snip off a corner to pipe on eyes, add details to flowers, or even add a pacifier to a baby pop. Make sure to use microwave-safe bags so that the chocolate can be stored and reused in them. The 3 × 5 inch poly bags sold to cover cake pops are the ideal bags to use, as they hold up well to the heat of a microwave and are not too thin.

Fondant

A box of fondant should always be kept in your pantry for cake pops. You can use it for everything from flowers to ears and to add texture to your pops. It is best used underneath chocolate to add details and as support for when you need something stable enough to handle the weight of the chocolate. It is also great to create depth in your pops and accents to go on top. Fondant is an under-utilized aspect of cake pops due to the fact many people do not like the taste of commercial fondant. If you dislike the taste, try making marshmallow fondant (see page 70). It complements many cake pop flavors, especially chocolate cake; however, it does not dry as hard as traditional fondant does.

Royal icing

Although chocolate is very versatile, and many effects can be achieved with it, there are certain things chocolate cannot convey properly, and that is where royal icing comes into play. It can convey fluffiness and lightness when creating clouds, dollops of whipped cream, or icing on a cake. If you don't want to pipe details with chocolate and want better control, use royal icing with a #1 or #2 piping tip to create fine lines and details.

Edible markers

Edible markers are useful for fine lines and to add details on everything from chocolate to fondant. Not all edible markers will write on chocolate, so you will need to read the package—most can only write on fondant and royal icing. Always buy food-safe edible markers. Just because a marker is non-toxic does not mean it should be consumed. When storing your markers make sure to keep them tip-side down in the fridge to prevent the tips from drying out. If you have trouble getting them to write, chill your pops after dipping them, especially if you thin down your chocolate with oil, so the marker doesn't pull up the chocolate and clog the tip.

Luster and petal dust

These are available in a wide variety of colors and have many uses. Try using them dry and dust them on pops to add highlights and create shading on shaped pops. The use of luster dust will give your pops a pearly effect and allow them to sparkle in sunlight, giving them a glittering look that is perfect for a princess party or girls' night out. They can also be used for painting on details when mixed with lemon juice or vodka.

Sprinkles

You can never own too many sprinkles. Sprinkles are available in all sorts of colors and designs. There is a sprinkle for every holiday and special occasion on the market. You can use them underneath chocolate to add depth to your pops or on top as decorations. Sugar pearls are great for noses, confetti sprinkles for eyes, and hearts for bows and ears.

Candy

Candies are the most versatile edible item to use in cake pops. Disk-shaped candies make great ears for bears, while sphere-shaped candies are perfect for noses, and string candy can be used for handles and hair when needed. If you are using hard candies or too many sprinkles, they can take away from the texture and flavor of the cake pops. Always make it known what candies are used on your cake pops to avoid choking. There is nothing worse than biting into a cake pop expecting a lush, dense cake filling only to be greeted by a rock-hard piece of candy.

Cake Pop Basics ● ● ● ● ● ● ● ● ● ●

Cake pops are as much a science as they are an art form. Understanding the basic techniques will help you better understand the art of cake pops. It takes time and practice to master the craft of cake popping, but with a little patience and planning, you too can be making them like a professional. Every single step in the process of making cake pops will affect the overall outcome. Skipping a step or not properly planning ahead can cause a domino effect that will lead to less than desirable results.

The first and most important step in making cake pops is baking the cake. The cake is the foundation of a successful cake pop–making experience. The ideal cake for cake pops should be somewhat dense with some body to it and should be on the drier side. The cake should be slightly moist but not as moist as a traditional box cake, as you still want it to crumble. If you are making a cake from scratch, avoid any light and airy cakes, like angel food or sponge cake. A light and airy cake will tend to yield a spongy dough consistency when mixed with a binder, which is harder to sculpt than a dense cake.

Ideally you want to bake the cake the night before you plan on using it and let it fully cool overnight. Not only does that ensure that you have a fully cooled cake, it allows the cake to dry up slightly, which is beneficial if you created a light and moist cake. The lower the moisture content the better, as it allows you more control with the texture when the binder is added. By not allowing the cake to fully cool and dry slightly, when mixed with a binder the cake will have a spongy texture and will not have as big of a pronounced flavor profile, as the binder gives the cake most of its flavor. The drier the cake is when mixed with a binder the better, as it will yield a less creamy product; however, do not use old, stale cake.

Although you might be under the impression you need to use frosting, it is not a necessary ingredient. Most boxed cakes will bind together without the use of frosting. If you are making a fruit-based cake like strawberry cake, the majority of the time a binder is not needed due to the high moisture content from the added fruit. If your cake is high in moisture it is best to opt out of adding a binder, but the flavor will be lacking. The use of frosting with a highly moist cake creates a variety of issues. When combined, the cake will be too soft and moist to roll into a perfectly shaped ball. The cake won't maintain its shape when rolled and will have the tendency to fall off the sticks when being dipped. It will also have a gummy texture.

If you opt out of using frosting or any binder, the best way to bind the cake is with a food processor. The food processor will blend it together until it is smooth; however, it will not create crumbs and the cake will be creamier in texture than what you would normally get when mixing with a stand mixer or with your hands. Cakes with naturally high moisture content like fruit based cakes can be bound together just by mixing by hand or with a stand mixer when mixed long enough. When opting out of a binder, it is easier to bind your cakes while still warm. The heat from a warm cake will supply moisture for the cake without the use of an additional binder.

Now, if you plan on using homemade cake or cakes with a much lower moisture content, you will need a binder. Any liquid, frosting, or edible paste will do. You can use frosting, peanut butter, marshmallow fluff, fruit puree, any jam of your liking, and even water or juice if needed.

To crumble the cake, start off mixing it with the paddle attachment on a stand mixer without any frosting or binder. Keep the mixer on low speed and allow the cake to fully crumble. When the crumbs look like sand, slowly add spoonfuls of the frosting or binder one at a time. As the cake is mixed with the binder, it will start to form tighter crumbs and will eventually come together into a tight dough-like mixture. Once it starts to pull away from the sides of the mixer, it is ready. Depending on the cake, sometimes you will have to stop the mixer and test it for consistency after each addition of the binder. Some cakes will never form a tight crumb or pull away from the sides of the mixer. It will still look dry even if a

binder is added, so you will have to test the consistency of it.

To test if the cake is ready, knead it a few times on a countertop and roll some of the cake mixture in your hands. If it falls apart, you need to

add more of the binder. The cake is ready once it holds its shape when rolled, and it should be firm in texture. The dough should feel slightly firmer than children's play dough. A three-to-one ratio is a good guide to go by when using a homemade cake. If you are using nine ounces of cake, you can expect to use at least three ounces of frosting. Always start off with less frosting than expected. You can always add more if needed, but you cannot take it away if too much is added.

Once you are ready to roll the balls, hand weigh each one to a one-ounce portion. A one-ounce cake ball will yield a pop that can be consumed in about two bites and is about one-and-a-half inches in diameter, the perfect size for a single person to enjoy. Place the dough in the palm of your hands while applying pressure and rotate your hands in a circular motion. As it starts to form a ball, gently relieve the pressure while maintaining the circular motion until your palms are barely touching it. If you end up with a rounded diamond shape, your cake is too moist. If you are working with a very firm, dense cake, moisten your hands to help with the rolling process. Lightly moistened hands will also help smooth out any surface cracks or blemishes the cake might have when rolled. During this process you will need to clean your hands, as the cake residue will build up.

Once you have completed rolling all the balls, chill them slightly in the fridge if needed. While the cake balls are chilling, prepare the chocolate for dipping. A pound of chocolate will cover around two dozen cake pops depending on the consistency of the chocolate. The thinner the consistency the more pops it will cover. When melting

chocolate, start off with melting only 75 percent of the chocolate you plan on using. Melt the chocolate in the microwave for thirty seconds and stir when finished. After the first thirty seconds, continue to melt in fifteen-second intervals, stirring after every interval to prevent overcooking. Once the majority of the chocolate has melted, add the remaining chocolate and mix it together. Let it sit for a bit, as the residual heat will soften the chocolate and allow it to cool slightly so that it doesn't overheat. Melt for an additional fifteen seconds to remove any final lumps. Different brands of chocolate will melt at different rates so keep an eye on it while in the microwave.

When the chocolate is ready and fully melted, dip the tips of the lollipop sticks into the chocolate and insert them halfway into the cake balls; allow to set before dipping. The chocolate will act as glue and keep the pop on the stick. You can wipe away the excess chocolate that pools up underneath the cake if desired. That ring of chocolate will stabilize the pop and prevent it from changing position while tapping off any excess chocolate left there. It will also prevent the cake from sliding down the stick after being dipped. After all the sticks have been inserted into the pops, it is time to thin down the chocolate if it is too thick. You can use cooking oil, shortening, or paramount crystals to thin down your chocolate.

The chocolate should be fluid enough to coat a spoon without the edges of the metal showing through the chocolate. If you can see the metal of the spoon after being coated, your chocolate is too thin. If the chocolate clings to the spoon in an uneven manner, the chocolate is too thick and will have to be thinned down. The chocolate should fall in a smooth, steady stream when ready for dipping. After the chocolate has reached the desired consistency, test the chocolate's finish. Dip the spoon into the chocolate and allow it to set to see if there are any issues with discoloration or pitting. Pitting is when the chocolate dries with small tiny craters in the finish, which is often the result of too much fat being added to the chocolate. The chocolate should ideally be glossy or matte in color, depending on the brand. If there are a bunch of white spots, the chocolate has bloomed, which is often a result of improper storage. There is no way to fix blooming once it has happened. Blooming can sometimes be masked with the use of a large amount of candy color added to the melted chocolate. If the chocolate dries with a streaky finish, it was not stirred enough. The streaking is caused by the chocolate drying at different rates because the chocolate was at different temperatures.

After the chocolate has been thinned down and the finish has been tested, you are ready to dip the pops. Make sure the chocolate on the sticks has fully hardened and that the balls are not cold. If the balls are cold the chocolate coating on the pops will crack. In a swift, steady motion, dunk the pop in the chocolate and pull it right out. Position it at an angle over your dipping vessel and gently shake off any excess chocolate. When you notice the amount falling off begins to decrease, gently tap the pop edge of your vessel while rotating it to ensure an even coat and remove any final excess. Place in a Styrofoam or wooden stand to dry, and you are ready to decorate.

Preparing Pops Ahead of Time •••••••••••••

Preparing a large amount of cake pops can seem like a daunting task, but with a little bit of planning and organization you can go through them in no time. You can prepare pops up to a week in advance, as long as they are kept cold. Contrary to belief, a pop does not taste fresher if it was made on the same day. Once the cake has been dipped, it will not dry out or go stale overnight. In fact, some flavors taste better when made two to three days ahead of time. Cake pops can last up to two weeks depending on flavors and fillings. If you use fresh fruit inside, they will remain good only for a few days, since eventually the fruit will start to decompose and the high moisture content will cause mold to develop. But as long as the pops do not have any perishable ingredients, they will last well over a week. Using pre-made frosting will extend the life span of your cake pops, since the frosting does not spoil and is shelf stable. You could also use melted chocolate in place of frosting as the binder to increase the lifespan of the cake pops.

There are two different ways to approach the production of a large number of cake pops if you are working with limited time. Some people prefer to bake the cake, roll the balls, and freeze the cake balls until they are needed. To freeze the un-dipped balls, line a sheet pan with parchment paper and fill up the pan. Once the pan is full, freeze the cake balls for a few hours until firm, then place them in an airtight container or in a plastic bag and keep frozen until ready to use. The only downside of freezing the cake balls is they do tend to dry out and lose flavor if left in the freezer for a long period of time. The cake balls also tend to crack once the stick has been inserted because of the lower moisture content if they have been left in the freezer too long of a period of time.

The preferred method to keep the cake as fresh and flavorful as possible is to bake the cake the night before you plan on using it. Doing it the night before allows the cake not only to cool down completely before being mixed with the frosting, but also allows any excess moisture to dry out, giving you more control over the texture. The following morning, blend the cake with the frosting, place the cake filling in an airtight container or plastic bag, and refrigerate until ready to use. This is a good method to utilize if your cake is really dry because it gives the cake and frosting time to fuse. You can keep the cake filling in the fridge up to a week before it needs to be rolled. This way you have all the cake you need ready to go, which will speed up the process for large orders. If you have a vacuum sealer you can prepare your cake mixture and freeze it until needed. Thaw it completely and, if needed, refresh the cake mixture with frosting to restore the proper consistency.

Handling the production of a large number of cake pops requires the use of an assembly line. After you have your cake mixture prepared, separate it into one-ounce portions or the desired size, then roll them all into balls. You can roll out the balls the night before you plan on dipping them as long as you line them on a sheet pan and cover them in plastic wrap to keep them from drying out. Using two different stands to hold the pops helps speed up the process. Use one stand to hold un-dipped pops and the other to hold the dipped pops. Dip the sticks into the chocolate and insert them into the cake, then place in the stand to harden. Once they harden, dip the pops again and place in a separate stand to harden. When the pops have hardened, begin to decorate them. Instead of decorating each pop individually, decorate them all one step at a time before going on to the next step of decorating.

Once the cake is dipped into chocolate and decorated, you can freeze the pops, but you should do so with caution, as the chocolate can discolor and will sweat when removed from the freezer if it is too warm. It is best to only freeze leftover pops. However, you can put the decorated pops in the fridge for an extended period of time. To store your pops, individually wrap each one and place them in an airtight container in the fridge to prolong their freshness for upwards of two weeks. Cake pops will also last up to a week in room temperature, but the sticks will begin to yellow after a few days.

Inverted Cake Pops

Inverted cake pops are free standing and do not require a cake pop stand for display purposes. They are typically displayed on platters during events. Inverted cake pops are slightly more challenging to make than regular cake pops and come with their own unique set of issues. When making inverted cake pops, you essentially make them the same way as a traditional cake pop, but instead of placing them in a stand to dry, they get inverted and placed on wax paper to harden.

One of the biggest issues with inverted cake pops is the cake being exposed at the bottom. The same thing that happens with cake balls will happen with these. The cake ends up pushing the chocolate to the sides as it rests to harden, which exposes the cake while it dries. There are three ways to make sure you achieve perfect bottoms on your inverted cake pops. The simplest is to make them as you normally would, and once they dry, use melted chocolate to pipe a small dot on the exposed cake and set them back on wax paper to dry again. This method is quick and simple but can be time consuming, especially when working with large quantities.

Another widely popular method involves using candy melts or confectionary wafers, which are disk shaped. Ahead of time, line your tray with the candy melt disks so they are flat. Dip the pops as usual, but instead of placing the pops to dry directly on wax paper, place them on the candy melt disks. This will ensure you have a perfect bottom each time and no cake will be exposed.

The last method involves using a sheet pan that has been chilled. Place a sheet pan in the freezer for a few minutes until it is cold to the touch. Remove the pan from the freezer, line with wax paper, and place the dipped pops directly onto the pan. The cold pan will quickly harden the chocolate and prevent the bottoms from becoming exposed.

Another issue that is common with inverted cake pops is that they lose their perfect ball shape after having the stick inserted. This happens a lot because of the fact that most people jam the stick in while the cake ball is resting on the tray after being rolled. When the stick is inserted, the cake gets pushed down and the bottom becomes really flat. It is always best to use a dense chilled cake so that it holds its shape better. You could also hold each ball in your hand and gently twist the stick into the cake. If you jam the stick into the cake while it is resting on a tray, it's likely that it will fall off during dipping because the weight is no longer evenly distributed. If you dip the stick and then the cake in the melted chocolate, place it in a cake pop stand and allow to dry upright. This allows the melted chocolate to form a tighter bond with the cake.

When you go to dip the inverted pops, you will dip them just the same as a regular cake pop. To prevent chocolate from pooling up around the base, wipe a small amount of chocolate off of the base of the pop onto your dipping vessel. If you find your sticks are not perfectly vertical as you are dipping them, once you place them to dry, you can gently adjust the stick so that it is not off center.

Pop Tops • • • • • • • • • • • • • • • • •

Pop tops, cake truffles, or, if you prefer, plain old cake balls are often not approached with the same creativity as cake pops due to the difficulty in achieving a proper smooth coating on them. Unlike a cake pop's stick, which allows for easy dipping, a cake ball is on its own. If you ever made cake balls before, you know how challenging it can be to make a pretty cake ball, especially one with a custom design. But any pop, regardless of shape or design, can technically become a cake ball. All you have to do is create the design you want as a cake pop. Once it is hard and fully decorated, cut the chocolate with a knife where the stick meets the cake and twist it to gently remove it from the pop without damaging the design. Next, take the pop top to a heated pan on the stove. Place the hole flat on the pan and move in a circular pattern to melt the chocolate and cover the hole. Place on a silicon mat to cool and you have a foolproof, flawless custom cake ball. This method is great when working with shaped designs that are difficult to dip.

Another, more challenging, method is using a fork and knife. Place the cake ball at the edge of your fork and fully submerge it into the melted chocolate. You can also spoon the chocolate over the cake to ensure complete coverage. Gently tap off all the extra chocolate. Place the fork flush to a silicon mat and use the knife to slide the cake ball onto the mat to cool. Once it dries you can clean up the edges of the cake ball with a knife.

The last possible method for cake balls is to chill them ahead of time. Prepare the chocolate and insert a toothpick into your cake ball, dip it, and treat it as a cake pop. Once you remove the excess chocolate, transfer it to your silicon mat and let cool. Once it is fully cool, remove the toothpick and hide the hole it created with a drizzle of chocolate.

To prevent the silicon mat from leaving exposed cake at the bottom of cake balls, chill the sheet pan so the chocolate will harden as soon as the balls are placed on it. You can also pipe a chocolate dot on a silicon mat and place the balls on top to seal up the cake or pipe chocolate directly onto the bottoms after being dipped.

Cake Pucks • • • • • • • • • • • • • • • •

Cake pucks refer to any variation of cake ball, bite, or truffle that uses a mold to achieve its shape or design. Cake pucks are traditionally made using sandwich-cookie chocolate molds and get their name because they look like a hockey puck. Molds are sold in all sorts of different shapes and designs, so you are not just limited to the classic hockey puck shape, but that is the most versatile shape you can have, as it is a blank canvas. Using the classic puck shape you can turn cake bites into snowmen, beach balls, babies, and many other designs.

Using a mold is a quick and efficient way to mass produce large numbers of cake bites while making sure they are uniform and perfect each time. There are two main ways to fill the molds with your cake filling. The first involves filling the molds with the chocolate to the top of the mold; allow it to sit for a few minutes, then poor out the remaining melted chocolate into a bowl. This will leave you with thin layer of chocolate in the mold that has hardened, creating a shell for the cake. Stuff the cake mixture into the mold, leaving some room on the top to coat with chocolate.

Pour the chocolate on top and place the mold in the freezer until fully hardened. Then you can pop it out of the mold and have a perfectly smooth and shiny cake puck. Using the shell method is ideal if you also want to make a layered cake bite that has jam or cream in it.

Another method to fill the molds without having to create the shell first is to roll your dough mixture between two sheets of wax paper. You want to roll them as thick as a sandwich cookie or slightly thicker depending on the depth of your mold. Using a round cookie cutter, cut out circles that will fit into your mold. Fill the mold one third of the way up with chocolate and place the cake inside while the chocolate is still wet. Fill the mold with more chocolate until the cake is completely covered. Place in the fridge or freezer until hard and remove.

Homemade vs. Boxed Cake •••••••••••••••••••

There is often a lot of discussion of whether to use boxed cake mix or make a cake from scratch. Many people who are just entering the world of cake pops tend to use boxed cake mix because of how simple it is to prepare. The biggest benefit of using a mix is time. Most box cakes require as little as two to three ingredients, which are typically pantry staples. A homemade cake tends to be much more complicated and requires as many as six to seven ingredients, many of which you don't keep on hand all the time.

When it comes to shaping the cake into different designs, it is easier to do so with cake from a mix due to its really high moisture content. Many boxed mixes, after being baked, don't require much, if any, frosting. Boxed cake mixes also don't crumble as finely as a homemade cake, leaving them with a creamier texture, which allows the cake to be easily manipulated into various shapes.

But a huge drawback of a boxed mix is the texture and density. Since many boxed mixes produce highly moist cakes, when the cake is crumbled

and mixed together you end up with a really light and soft filling. If you are not careful, you can easily add too much frosting and end up with a mushy mess. Although that soft filling is great for sculpting, a lot of people do not like the texture. If you are going to use a box cake you should allow it plenty of time to dry and cool down after baking. Ideally allow the cake to dry overnight if possible. You should also limit or scale back the liquid ingredients in the recipe. Try adding less oil or water than required and avoid purchasing cakes with pudding in the mix. When possible, purchase cake mixes that call for butter instead of oil, as this will help cut back on the moistness.

Homemade cakes tend to be drier than boxed mixes, but they will yield cake pops with much better texture. Using a drier cake allows you more control in the finished product and gives you the chance to use various flavored binders to enhance the flavor of the pop. Cake pops made from scratch tend to have a dense, cake-like texture and crumble easily. The flavor is often bolder and more pronounced. Working with a homemade cake does take some time to get used to since the dough tends to be stiffer. Failing to add the proper amount of frosting will yield balls that will crumble in your hands while rolling.

In the end it comes down to personal preference. Box cakes are simple to make and easier to sculpt, whereas a homemade cake has a more pronounced flavor and maintains its shape better. If you plan ahead, go with the homemade cake for better flavor and texture, but if you are in a bind you can use a boxed mix cake.

Flavoring the Cake • • • • • • • •

Cake itself is such a versatile dessert with a wide variety of flavors and combinations that the possibilities for cake pops are endless. Never limit your cake choices to just chocolate and vanilla. You can be as adventurous and bold as you like with cake pops.

There are three main components when it comes to flavoring cake pops: the cake, the binder, and the mix-ins. First you have the cake, or your base. The easiest way to flavor cake batter is with extracts, fruit purees, syrups, or juice. You can also use crushed cookies, Jell-O, or candies.

As the cake bakes, some of the flavor weakens, and that is where the binder comes into play. The binder usually adds the most flavor to the cake pops. You can use anything from frostings to edible creams and jams. If you plan on using a butter cream as the binder, you want to make it slightly stronger than you normally would so that when it is mixed with the cake you have an intense flavor. Generally it is best to match your binder to the cake flavor—if you are making a peanut butter cake, you want to use peanut butter frosting.

You can also flavor your cake pops with mix-ins, which can be anything from fresh fruit to chopped nuts and candies. If you are going to use fruit, chop it into small pieces and squeeze out any excess moisture. Any pops with fresh fruit will have a limited shelf life, as the fruit will decompose and can get moldy. If you plan on using mix-ins that are hard or crunchy, like nuts or cookies, make sure to finely chop them, otherwise you won't be able to roll a smooth ball and the stick will move around when you dip the pops.

You can mix and match flavors to create a wide variety of cake pops. Mix a cinnamon graham cracker cake with marshmallow fluff and mini chocolate chips for s'more cake pops. Or you can use the same flavor for the cake, binder, and mix-ins—bake the cake with crused Oreos, use an Oreo butter cream, and mix in crushed Oreos for an intense cookies-and-cream flavor. The possibilities are endless when coming up with new cake pop flavors.

Colored Cakes and Designs · · · · · · · · · · · · · ·

Not only are cake pops customizable on the outside, you can also customize the inside to make them uniquely creative. By coloring the cake batter before it is baked, you can match your cake pops to different themes and events. You can add pink and blue colors to a white or yellow cake base for baby showers, or red and green for Christmas. Instead of red velvet cake try making blue or green velvet cake.

With colored cakes you can create everything from solid-color cake pops to marbled effects and even rainbow or striped cake. After you color the cake batter, bake it as you normally would. Adding too much food coloring will give the cake a metallic taste. Once it fully cools, mix it with frosting to prepare the dough mixture. You can use one color to create solid-color cakes or use multiple colors to create a marbled effect.

There are two methods for creating marbled cake. The first involves using two equal portions of different colored cake and slightly mixing them together before rolling. As you roll the cake, the two colors will swirl together. This method is best when you want the colors to remain distinct and

vibrant. The second method involves kneading two or more different colored cakes until the colors are finely swirled together, then weighing off one-ounce portions and rolling. This will result in more of a subtle, intertwined swirl. For rainbow cake pops you want to use four to five different colors. Pinch off a little portion of cake from each of the colored cake mixtures, stack them on top of each other, and roll them together. It's good to stack different colored cakes if working with four or more colors because they remain separated and distinct when you roll them together.

If you plan on using a cookie cutter as a mold for your cake pops, you can also create a striped cake pattern. Using two or more different colors, you are going to push the cake into the cookie cutter in layers. Stack the cakes in even layers until the cutter is fully packed, then remove it from the cookie cutter. If you don't want to apply each layer by hand, place some of the cake mixture in between parchment paper and roll out thinly. Stack the layers on top of each other and cut out the shapes using the cookie cutter.

You can apply these methods to create a variety of fun cake pops. Using solid blue or pink cake, you can create gender reveal pops for a baby shower. Mixing red cake with mini chocolate chips and dipping in green chocolate creates a watermelon pop. Or layer black and white cake for zebra pops—the possibilities are endless.

Types of Chocolate •••••••••

The type of chocolate you use can make or break your cake pop experience when making them for the first time. It is the most important aspect of cake pops. There are many options available on the market, which can make the whole process overwhelming. Currently, the most common types of chocolate that stores carry fall into three categories. First you have candy melts, also known as confectionery wafers, which come as round, colored disks, generally in one-pound bags. The second type available is almond bark, which comes in the form of big bars weighing more than a pound. Lastly, you have common baking chocolate, like chocolate chips and bars. They are generally sold in bags or bars weighing around twelve ounces for bags or four to six ounces for bars.

Candy melts are the most popular type used for cake pops, since they do not need to be tempered and, when dried, will be much harder and more durable than a regular baking chocolate will be. They come pre-colored, so you are limited in color choices, but you can always add candy color or any oil-based food color to brighten them up. Candy

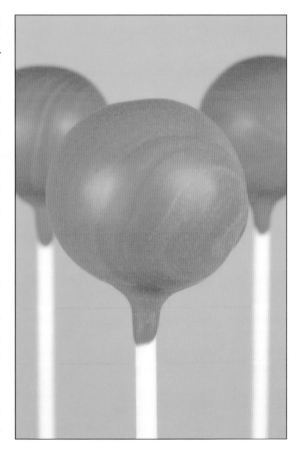

melts can be found in most craft and hobby stores, as well as online. Each brand of candy melts has a different consistency when melted, and it is important to know that difference before dipping your cake pops. Some brands work better than others do in specific weather and environments. You want to use a brand that best fits where you live. Try to use a chocolate that falls off of your spoon in a silky smooth stream when melted. Most brands of candy melts do require thinning down to achieve a fluid consistency that is acceptable for dipping.

Candy melts can sometimes easily overcook in the microwave and then crystallize. Once the candy melts have crystallized they will become grainy and lumpy. Because of their quarter-sized disk shape, the chocolate is more exposed to the heat of the microwave, so it takes less time for it to melt compared to almond bark. If you are not paying attention to it the chocolate can overheat, which can make chocolate too thick for dipping, as well as make it crystallize. Another common issue is the chocolate blooming during transit from factory to store. When the chocolate is stored in conditions over 75°F, some of the fat becomes visible on the surface, which is seen as white spots once it hardens. It is a purely cosmetic issue and does not affect the flavor.

Almond bark is the second-most popular choice and can only be found only as vanilla or chocolate. Almond bark works just as wonderfully as candy

melts do; nearly all brands on the market tend to melt silky smooth with no need to be thinned down. They also give you more control with color designs since you are working with a blank canvas. They come in brick form, which allows you to take as much or as little as needed. What is also great about almond bark is that blooming is rare and mainly affects the smaller bars and disk types of chocolate. The brands of almond bark that include a melting tray typically melt the smoothest and are the best tasting. The only downside is that cheap almond bark can have a grainy feel and is not as sweet as candy melts are. If you like, you can mix almond bark with candy melts to help balance each other out.

Candy melts and almond bark are not, in fact, real chocolate. Chocolate has cocoa butter in it and requires tempering to provide a shine and snap to it. Tempering chocolate is the process of heating and cooling chocolate to control the crystallization of cocoa butter. Candy melts and almond bark have the cocoa butter replaced by another type of fat, traditionally vegetable oil, which allows you to skip the whole tempering process. In some areas and parts of the globe you cannot find almond bark or candy melts.

The last type of chocolate you can use is traditional baking chocolate. This is great if you are in a bind since it is readily available at most stores. However, it tends to require much more work than the others since it requires tempering and costs more per pound. In order to use any real chocolate, it is best to temper it first. This process is needed to produce a firm, glossy chocolate with a good snap to it. To temper chocolate, start off by setting up a double boiler. Chop your chocolate and melt two-thirds of it in the double boiler, constantly stirring. Heat it until it reaches 110°F for milk or white chocolate, or 115°F for dark chocolate.

Once it reaches the proper temperature, remove the bowl from the heat and add the remaining chocolate, stirring until the temperature drops back down to 80–82°F. Place the bowl back over the heat and reheat until you reach 86–88°F for milk and 88–89°F for dark chocolate. Once at the desired temperature, you are ready to dip.

If you are wondering whether you can use chocolate chips as the coating, the answer is yes and no. The majority of brands available on the market tend to have an additive in them that helps the chocolate maintain its shape at high temperatures. So by the time they finally melt smoothly the chocolate will have overheated and missed the proper tempering temperatures. You can technically use it, but it will never be as hard as candy melts or almond bark are and will be soft to the touch. So the pops would not be strong enough if they needed to be shipped.

Melting and Storing Chocolate • • • • • • • • • • • • • • • •

A key step in making cake pops is melting the chocolate. Failing to properly melt the chocolate can cause a variety of issues. To melt the chocolate you have two main options. The first option is the double-boiler method. Heat a pot with about an inch or two of water to a simmer and place a heat-proof bowl on top, so that it is being heated by the steam. Place the chocolate inside the bowl and slowly keep stirring until it is melted. The double-boiler method is the safer of the two methods to use, but it is much more time consuming and requires your constant attention.

The other, more popular method is with a microwave. The microwave is the quickest method to use when melting chocolate. Pour 75 percent of the chocolate you plan on melting into a bowl and microwave it for thirty seconds. Once the thirty seconds are up, stir so the chocolate doesn't get unevenly heated. Put it in for another fifteen seconds, then continue melting the chocolate in fifteen-second intervals until smooth.

Once smooth, add the remaining 25 percent of chocolate and stir. Let it rest on the counter for a

few minutes to soften the newly added chocolate. (The reason to melt only 75 percent of the chocolate, then add the remaining 25 percent, is so that the chocolate does not overheat. Adding the remaining 25 percent of the chocolate will cool it down, especially if it is close to becoming overcooked.) After the chocolate has softened, place it back in the microwave and heat until fully melted. If you have any stubborn lumps of chocolate that won't melt, you can use an immersion blender to break up those chunks or strain them out with a fine mesh strainer. When melting chocolate keep in mind some brands will melt at different rates, so always keep an eye on it.

If the melted chocolate is thick and not fluid, it could be the brand, as some naturally melt into a thick consistency. Heating it up more will not make it any thinner. Too much time in the microwave will overheat it and make it thicker. Overheated chocolate will be slightly thick and appear cracked and separated when on a pop. An easy way to tell if the chocolate is overheated is to scoop it up with a spoon and allow it to fall back into the bowl. When it falls back into the bowl, the spoon will have layers of chocolate appearing as if it cracked and separated.

If you feel that the chocolate is on the verge of becoming overheated, add un-melted chocolate, which will help balance out the heat and cool it down. If you did overheat your chocolate, you can

save it by thinning it down and allowing it to cool. The perfect consistency for dipping should be fluid enough to coat a spoon without the edges of the metal showing through the chocolate, as well as fall back into the bowl in a smooth, steady stream.

If you can see the metal of the spoon after being coated, your chocolate is too thin. If the chocolate needs to be thinned down, make sure the type of fat you use is waterless. Do not use butter or margarine, which contain water. Cooking oil, shortening, or paramount crystals all work perfectly fine. Avoid using olive oil, due to the taste it leaves behind, or nut oils, in case of allergies. Make sure to fully mix the fat into the chocolate before dipping, otherwise the pops will have a streaky, glossy finish to them when dried.

A small amount of oil can go a long way. Start with less than a teaspoon and gradually add more until you reach the desired consistency. If you add too much oil, it will weaken the chocolate and take much longer to set. Sometimes if you go overboard with the oil, it will not set and will remain soft to the touch. Your pops will also have a spotted crater-like texture once dried if too much oil was added, which is known as pitting. If you don't want to thin down the chocolate, the thick chocolate works wonders for creating details and accents for the pops.

When it comes to storing the chocolate, you want to keep it in a cool, dry place. Storing chocolate in a damp environment will cause the chocolate to bloom. After you have dipped all your pops and have finished with the chocolate, make sure to strain it in a fine mesh strainer. This removes crumbs and chocolate lumps that might be remaining, as well as any stray candies or sprinkles used in decorating that might have fallen in. You have two main options for storing the chocolate. The most popular method is to store the chocolate in the containers that pre-made frosting comes in. Those containers

are microwave-safe, stackable, and easy to store. Those containers are also the perfect size for a dipping vessel, so there is no cleanup. Use the ones with a clear lid so you can see which container has which color. Always label or mark the container if the chocolate has come in contact with nut products in case of allergies.

If you don't want to melt a whole container of chocolate, especially when you only need a little of one color, you can also pour the melted chocolate into small silicon molds and store them in air-tight containers. This allows you to pick and choose the amount needed instead of melting a large batch of chocolate. The difference between storing it in a container as a large mass and storing it in small molded shapes depends on when you melt it.

When you re-melt the chocolate, there are two typical outcomes. When you store your chocolate as a large block, it tends to melt much better than when storing as smaller blocks. Melting smaller chunks of chocolate exposes them to more heat, and the consistency might become thick. But if you don't stir the large blocks of chocolate in the frosting containers, most of the heat ends up focused on the bottom, which causes the chocolate to crystallize. Once chocolate has crystallized, there is no saving it, even if you strain.

Coloring Chocolate · · · · · · · ·

The majority of the time when working with cake pops, you will have to make and mix custom colors. If the chocolate you are using is not pre-colored, you can color it on your own. There are two ways to color chocolate. The most popular way is with candy color, which is an oil-based food color. You can also use powdered food coloring. Do not use water-based color or gel color, as those will seize your chocolate and render it useless. Seizing occurs when liquid is added to chocolate while it is melted, which causes it to harden and become unable to properly melt again. Oil-based colors are great because they come in a wide variety of colors and are potent.

The only downside to candy color, besides its staining ability if spilled, is that specific colors tend to thicken the chocolate quickly. Colors like yellow, orange, blue, and green will make your chocolate too thick to dip into when added in large amounts. When dealing with a color like orange, it is best to use yellow as a base for the chocolate and add the orange to it. It is also easier to use pre-colored candy melts if possible as the

base and add small amount of candy color until you achieve the desired shade. If the chocolate ends up too thick due to large amounts of added color, thin it down with cooking oil. Another good thing about candy color is that a little goes a long way with some colors. A little drop of pink into white can give you a bright hot pink in seconds; the more used, the brighter the color gets. If you add too much of other colors—for example, red or black—they will alter the taste of the chocolate, giving you a bitter, metallic taste.

The other option is powdered food color. It is recommended to blend powdered food color into oil before adding it to chocolate, which allows it to be mixed in evenly. This also allows the chocolate to accept the color easier. The downside of powdered color is that it takes a lot more of it to color chocolate, and it's not as potent as its commercially available oil-based counterparts. You can find most colors as oil-based; however, neon and metallic colors are not sold in oil-based form. If the color you need is not sold in an oil-based form, you can always boost the color after it has dried with petal or luster dust. You can achieve silver or gold pops by dry dusting them with silver or gold luster dust after the chocolate has hardened or spray them with edible luster spray.

To color the chocolate, dip a toothpick into the color, then stir it into the chocolate. Doing it this way allows you to have better control of the color's

intensity than if you poured it in a drop at a time. If you pour the color in you can easily add too much color. After you have successfully colored the chocolate, keep in mind that some colors will intensify as they sit. You should color your chocolate one shade lighter than needed and allow the

achieve. If you need to use black for a pop, start off with dark chocolate as your base. Dark chocolate meant specifically for candy fountains works best because it is naturally fluid when melted and does not need to be thinned down. To achieve black, you can use black candy color with some purple added; the addition will intensify the black color of the chocolate. When wet, the chocolate will have a blackish purple hue to it, but once it dries it will be jet black. You can also mix red with black. If you don't have black candy color on hand you can use blue and purple with dark chocolate. Avoid using light colors like pink, yellow, or orange. When coloring chocolate black, it can require a lot of food coloring, which can thicken the chocolate to a frosting-like consistency if too much is added. In that case, you can thin it down with cooking oil. The main downside of using black for a cake pop is that it can stain your mouth if too much food coloring is added. If you are going to use black for cake pops, make it an accent color and not the base color.

Creating a flesh-toned pop can be done in numerous ways. The first is with peanut butter candy melts. Melt the peanut butter–flavored candy melts and add white or milk chocolate as needed to achieve the skin tone desired. However, with the amount of peanut allergies nowadays, many people cannot use peanuts. You can also use butterscotch-flavored candy melts, but it

chocolate to sit for a few minutes to ensure that it won't intensify. Make sure to fully stir in the color to avoid different-colored streaks on the pops.

Black and flesh tones are two of the most popular colors that can be difficult to properly is an acquired taste. The best and easiest method for achieving a peach skin tone is mixing even portions of white, pink, and yellow candy melts by weight or volume. Add a few chips of regular chocolate to darken the flesh tone if needed. You can also start off with white chocolate as your base and add very small amounts of milk chocolate to it until you achieve the desired color for a tan flesh tone. There are even some brands of pre-colored pink candy melts that are so light in color that with the addition of white candy melts you can create a peach flesh tone.

Shaping Cake Pops ● ● ● ● ● ● ● ●

The novelty of cake pops is in being able to turn cake into uniquely shaped edible art. Sometimes there are shapes we just cannot create by using our hands, but you can always use cookie cutters. They are a cake pop maker's best friend, as they allow you to achieve new and exciting shapes that were unachievable before.

Small cookie cutters, two inches or smaller in size, make for great molds. You want to use cutters that are at least ⅝ of an inch tall. Small cookie cutters can hold anywhere from 1.5 ounces to under an ounce of cake depending on the size of the cutter. Removing the cake from them can be quite challenging if you are not prepared. If you have trouble removing the cake from a cookie cutter, keep a bowl of water next to you and place the cookie cutter inside. Lightly dampen your hands, remove the cutter from the water, and place on a flat surface. Stuff the cutter with cake and gently push the shape out, starting from any sharp point. The water will act as a lubricant and allow it to easily slide out. Once removed, flip the shape over and lightly tap the surface of it with the palm of

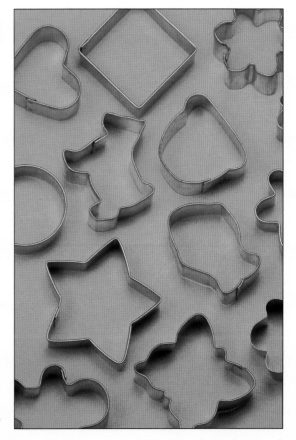

your hand to flatten out all the indentations you created while removing the shape. If you are having trouble with removing the cake, chilling the dough ahead of time makes this process easier.

When you create a shape by hand, all the edges are naturally round, so the chocolate clings to it, but once you use a cookie cutter as a mold, you are left with sharp edges of cake that become visible after being dipped. To prevent this you can use a light-color cake, smooth out the edges, or double dip. To smooth out the edges, flatten all the sharp edges with your fingertips. Flattening the entire pop with the palm of your hand or the bottom of a flat surface will also round out the edges and give you a wider surface area for decorating.

Now that you have a shaped pop, inserting the stick can be troublesome depending on the thickness of the cake. If you insert the stick and notice cracks where it has gone through, pipe chocolate along the lines and smooth it over to add support to the shape. To avoid those cracks, hold the shape in the center with your fingers and gently insert while twisting the stick. The cracks will appear if the cake mixture is not moist enough or the cake is not thick enough for the stick to be inserted.

If you used a cookie cutter as a mold or a dark-colored cake, double dipping your cake pops is a great method to hide sharp edges, as it hides all blemishes and prevents the cake from showing through, which gives you a more polished

looking pop. If you are going to double dip your pops, make sure the chocolate is fluid and much thinner than you would normally use. If you don't thin down the chocolate, the second coat will be too heavy and the cake will fall off of the stick.

You can also shape pops by hand if you don't want to use cookie cutters. When shaping pops by hand you can shape them in 3D or 2D. Take a baseball cake pop, for example. You could roll your cake into round, sphere-shaped balls, or you can make them into flat, round circles. The benefit of shaping the pops in 2D as a flat, round circle is that you are given a wider surface area for decorating. It is also easier to pipe straight lines and other details without the shape and design getting distorted. If the pop is flat, after all the details have been added or piped on it can dry lying down so you avoid the risk of the chocolate starting to run, as with a 3D pop.

Chilling Before Dipping ••••

Chilling your pops before dipping is a personal choice that should be made based off of the cake you use. If you are using a cake that is really soft and has a high moisture content, you should chill the pops before dipping so they retain their shape and stay on the stick. But if you use a dense cake, especially a homemade one, chilling is not needed. A dense chocolate cake does not require chilling, whereas a vanilla cake does, since it is softer in texture and has a higher chance of falling off of the stick.

The main benefit of chilling the pops is that they become firm and won't fall into the chocolate. Chilling is also beneficial when working in summer heat as it allows the pops to set much faster. But if your pops are too cold, the chocolate will set before it has the chance to evenly smooth out. If you chill the cake mixture before rolling, it will make the cake easier to handle. You should also chill the cake mixture if you plan on using a cookie cutter as a mold so the cake will be firm and easier to push out from the cutter.

The main downside of chilling is the pops cracking. As the pops chill they will shrink slightly, so

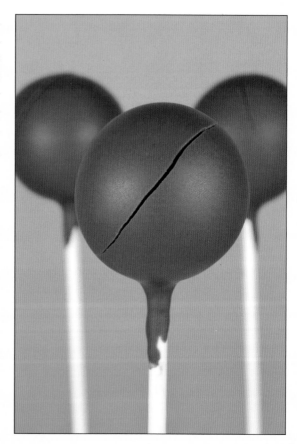

when they start to return to room temperature the cake will expand and try to force its way out. The pressure will build up and cause the chocolate to crack or split in any weak spots. This can be a nightmare, especially after you have decorated your cake pops, and sometimes it can take up to thirty minutes before they crack. To avoid this, make sure that you let them come to room temperature before dipping and that your chocolate is cool to the touch. You never want to dip a cold cake ball in hot chocolate. The cake can be cool to the touch but not cold. You can also experience cracking if you pipe on details or a design with chocolate that is too hot if the cake was chilled before dipping.

If you are making inverted cake pops, you can dip them after chilling without worrying about them cracking; when they rest on a silicon mat or parchment paper, the bottom of the cake will be exposed, which will alleviate the pressure.

To fix cracked pops, you can either pipe melted chocolate into the crack or smooth it out, or you can also double dip. If you are going to double dip the pops, allow the pops to rest before dipping a second time so that the cake will shrink and close the gap created by the cracked chocolate.

Pops Falling Off During Dipping ● ● ● ● ● ● ● ● ● ● ● ● ● ● ● ●

If you find yourself with a batch of cake pops that keep falling off of the sticks while dipping, various things can be the cause. If the cake is too wet when you insert the stick, the chocolate will have nothing to cling on to and the pop will not be stable enough for dipping. The moisture will create a barrier between the chocolate and cake, preventing it from sticking. Always make sure to use a cake that is not too moist and is fairly dense before dipping.

Pops can also fall off and slide down the sticks if you don't let the chocolate that was coated onto the stick set before dipping. That chocolate acts as both glue and support for the cake and prevents it from falling off and sliding.

Another issue is pop weight. The ideal size is one ounce of cake filling. If you try making a pop that is over two ounces, the weight of the pop and chocolate will cause it to fall off. Sometimes if you push your stick too far up into the cake, the weight of the chocolate will cause the cake to slide and break after being dipped. Make sure to never stick it in further than halfway. If you used a cookie cutter as a mold and the cake had cracks in it from the stick being inserted, the cake will crack and break after being dipped. That is why any cracks need to be patched up.

Chocolate is another culprit. If you attempt to dip in chocolate that is too thick, the cake will fall off due to the weight of the chocolate. Always use a fluid chocolate when dipping and gently tap off any excess chocolate.

Smooth Cake Pops • • • • • • • •

Achieving perfectly smooth pops takes time and practice, but with a few helpful tips you will be on your way. It all begins with the base. Remember that when you go to dip any pop, whether a round ball or a shape, the chocolate will cover every nook and cranny of the cake. If the ball of cake starts off lumpy or with cracks and creases in it, the end result will show that. You have to make sure you have the correct cake consistency for rolling.

First, make sure that you don't add too much frosting or binder to the cake mixture. Always start to mix the cake without frosting, then slowly add frosting or a binder a little at a time until it binds together. The cake filling should be slightly stiff, like children's clay, but pliable. The cake-to-frosting ratio that generally works is 3 to 1. If you add too much frosting or the cake is too moist to begin with, you will end up with mushy dough that won't maintain its shape. Remember, less is more when it comes to frosting. If it is too sticky, you can always add more cake to it or roll pops when the cake is chilled to help achieve a smooth ball.

When working with a drier cake, a splash of water on your hands works wonders, especially when dealing with homemade cakes or altered boxed cakes. Both tend to be harder to roll and tend to crack if you don't have enough frosting. The outer crumb layer will loosen, which will make a smoother ball as it moves around in the palms of your hands.

If, when rolling, you keep getting rounded, cone-shaped ends on your ball, either your hands or the cake are too wet. To fix that, dry your hands and start over or add more cake to your mixture. Once you have a rounded ball, gently shape any minor imperfections on it with your fingertips to create an even sphere.

The last key step is to use fluid chocolate. If the chocolate is thick it will be much harder to get a smooth-looking pop, and it will generally fall off the stick. To see if your chocolate is fluid enough, scoop some up with a spoon and let it fall back into your bowl. It should fall in a steady stream. If the chocolate is too thick and plops back into the bowl, you can adjust the consistency with cooking oil, shortening, or paramount crystals. Never dip the pops in chocolate that has been overheated, as the pops will not have a smooth finish. If you dip the pops in overheated chocolate without letting it cool or thinning it down first, the chocolate will begin to fall and will appear as if cracking off in layers.

When dipping the cake pops, make sure the chocolate is in a deep enough container so that the cake can be completely submerged. Pre-made frosting containers are ideal dipping vessels. Fully submerge the pop into the chocolate, pull it up quickly, hold it at a forty-five-degree angle, and gently shake it side to side so that the chocolate from the top slides and falls off the bottom. After you have most of the chocolate off, gently tap it on the dipping vessel while rotating to remove all the excess chocolate and smooth it out.

When dipping a shaped pop, each pop will have a positive side and a negative side. The positive side is the presentation side and the back is the negative. Hold the pop so that the positive side faces you and tap your wrist with your free hand to tap off any excess chocolate to make sure you get a smooth finish. The back side will have what we call the drip line. Drip lines are what forms when the chocolate falls back into the bowl, creating lines and ridges of chocolate on the pop. Once the positive side is smooth and no more chocolate is falling into the bowl, flip the pop over with the negative side facing you and gently shake the pop from left to right, allowing the chocolate to smooth out on the back side of the pop to remove any drip lines. If the pop you are dipping has a flat back, you can wipe away any excess chocolate onto the dipping vessel, which will help smooth it out and prevent chocolate from sliding down the stick.

Decorating and Painting Cake Pops ● ● ● ● ● ● ● ● ● ● ● ● ●

Cake pops are edible art on a stick and are as cute as they are delicious. They may seem daunting to make for someone just starting out, as they offer endless possibilities. The only limit is your imagination! You can decorate cake pops with a variety of edible items, including sprinkles, cookies, candies, frosting, and chocolate. Cake pop decorating combines two of the most common pastry art forms: cake and sugar cookie decorating.

When creating a cake pop, you are essentially making a mini, scaled-down cake. You should approach each cake pop as if it were both a cake and a sugar cookie. Focus on creating the basic shape and structure as if you were creating a cake, but treat the decor as if it were a sugar cookie. You have many options when it comes to decorating cake pops. You can create designs and features with sprinkles or candies, or pipe, paint, or draw on all the details.

There are two distinct style of decorating cake pops. The European style of cake pops tends to involve painted pops, whereas the classic, traditional style involves decorating details with

chocolate, candies, and sprinkles. Europeans tend to paint on all the details using either cocoa butter or petal dust and edible leaf glaze. You can purchase cocoa butter already colored or in white and color it yourself with powdered food coloring. You need to melt the cocoa butter and color it if not already colored. Using a fine-tipped, soft-bristle paintbrush, paint on all the details. After you have painted the pops, you have to set them in the fridge so the cocoa butter can set once again. It will take a few minutes to harden until it is no longer sticky.

You can also use edible leaf glaze, which is a 50/50 blend of confectioner's glaze and a food-grade Isopropyl alcohol, making sure to allow the pops to air dry after painting. In some countries, you can only find confectioner's glaze. Confectioner's glaze is a food-grade refined, bleached lacquer that is used to give items a glossy finish. There are two main issues when working with confectioner's glaze. The first is the smell of it; it has a very strong odor since it is a bleached lacquer. If you are going to use confectioner's glaze you will need to cut it 50/50 with either an extract with a high alcohol content or flavorless vodka. If you don't like the smell of the glaze, cut it with a strongly scented extract, which will mask the odor. It is also very sticky when wet and hard to remove from paintbrushes and surfaces once dried. This is another reason for cutting it with an extract or flavorless vodka. Alcohol helps it become less sticky and easier to remove. Household cleaners will not remove confectioner's glaze from surfaces or paintbrushes, which is why you need to purchase the glaze thinner as well. Confectioner's glaze thinner is a blend of acetate, acetone, and alcohol.

You need to add a drop at a time of the 50/50 blend to petal dust or powdered food coloring and mix the two until it's thin enough to paint with. When working with a blend, the details painted on will dry quickly, as the alcohol evaporates and allows it to set quicker. If you use the glaze by itself to achieve a glossy finish, it will take some time for the pops to dry and not be tacky to the touch. If you can't find edible leaf glaze or confectioner's glaze, you can use petal dust and unflavored vodka or extract. The paint consistency will be a little thinner than if using the glaze and will be more matte in finish since the glaze adds shine.

If you don't like the idea of painting pops, you can decorate them using chocolate and sprinkles for most of the details. Using candies and sprinkles allows you to create all sorts of designs and patterns. Sprinkles are wonderful to use to create small details, especially if you are not used to piping. If you cannot find specific sprinkles, you can also pipe on all the details with melted chocolate or royal icing. Sprinkles can be attached to cake pops while the chocolate is both wet and dry. The easiest way to transfer a sprinkle to a pop without leaving fingerprints is with tweezers or a toothpick. If the sprinkle you want to attach is flat, tap the tip of a toothpick on the surface of the sprinkle. Since sprinkles are porous, the tip will get stuck to the sprinkle and the sprinkle will easily adhere to the pop.

Attaching sprinkles to wet chocolate is best if you need to ship the pops since they will be secured. Just make sure the sprinkles are not too heavy so they don't fall and slide down the pop. If needed, allow the chocolate to cool a bit before attaching them. If you want to attach the sprinkles or candies once the chocolate has hardened, all you need to do is dab on small dots of melted chocolate with a toothpick, place the sprinkles or candies on top, and allow to set.

It can be hard to add really fine details to the pops using only sprinkles, and that is where edible markers, chocolate, and royal icing come into play. You can draw any designs you wish with edible markers, but they can be tricky to use since they can dig up the chocolate. For best results, store the markers tip-side down in the fridge and chill the pops before using the marker on them. Make sure the brand you purchase will write on chocolate, as most edible markers are not designed for doing this.

If you want to avoid using markers, you can pipe on all the details with chocolate or royal icing. Piping is the preferred decorating method because

it is inexpensive, less time consuming, and uses the same chocolate as dipping. Chocolate details, unlike sprinkles, will not take away from the cake pop's texture. When piping chocolate, you need to make sure the chocolate is fluid and not too thick so that you have control over it. Consistency is key when using chocolate for decorating, just as when using royal icing when decorating sugar cookies.

There are three main consistencies to use when working with chocolate for piping. First is really fluid chocolate; with this consistency the chocolate should fall back into itself and not hold any shape whatsoever. This is perfect for flooding, as when creating the faces for a monkey cake pop. Using a really fluid-consistency chocolate is challenging for fine lines and details, for which you will want to use a medium-consistency chocolate. A medium consistency will slightly hold its shape. If you pipe it into a pile, the chocolate will slightly collapse on itself, but the individual lines of chocolate will be noticeable. Another consistency to use is a thick chocolate, which maintains shape after being piped and won't collapse on itself. You really want to use a thick consistency when creating textures like frosting, fur, or grass. The thick chocolate works wonders for piping a border on a cake or creating a grass skirt or even vines.

When working with chocolate that will be used to pipe on details, it is best to purchase the brands that will melt naturally thick. This way you can easily adjust the consistency to your liking for piping. To adjust the consistency, add cooking oil, shortening, or paramount crystals to thin down the chocolate. To pipe chocolate, melt it in a small plastic bag and snip the corner off of it. Try to snip

off a small corner—the smaller the hole, the more control you have over the thickness of your line. You can adjust the size of your lines with the size of the hole. When piping details on a pop, use a plastic bag filled with rice to keep the pop stationary. After you pipe on the details with chocolate, allow the pops to dry in a horizontal position or at a 30–45 degree angle depending on the design. Avoid placing them in an upright position until the chocolate has set so that the chocolate doesn't run and distort the shape of what was piped on.

Piping chocolate does require a steady hand, and if you are having trouble getting used to it, you can use royal icing instead. Use royal icing in a piping bag fitted with a number 1, number 2, or number 3 piping tip, depending on the desired thickness. Royal icing is more forgiving since you can easily wipe away any mistakes you make, unlike chocolate. Using a medium-consistency icing will give you the best control. If using royal icing, you should never bag the pops until it has fully hardened.

To practice piping details, on a sheet of paper trace the outline of various small cookie cutters. Place that sheet underneath wax paper and, using either chocolate or royal icing, practice decorating and piping in the small area to get used to working on a small surface.

Now, when making cake pops you do not have to focus on only doing custom shapes or designs. You can quickly and easily accent pops by drizzling round pops, or using sprinkles or chocolate molds to match your event's theme. Using fondant is wonderful for creating simple and effortless accents for pops. Simple accents can be created by using ¾-inch fondant cutters or jumbo sprinkles.

Drizzling also offers a quick and simple way to decorate large amounts of cake pops in little time. Not only is drizzling simple but it also helps cover blemishes and errors on cake pops. You can apply a top drizzle, full body drizzle, side swirl, and more. After the pops have dried, pick a different color of chocolate than the base coat and drizzle the chocolate back and forth over the top of the cake pop. To apply a full body drizzle to a cake pop, prepare candy melts in a plastic bag and snip off the corner. You are going to gently squeeze the bag while holding the cake pop in a horizontal position, and then rotate the stick between your fingers so the chocolate swirls around the entire pop.

Heat and Humidity •••••••

Whether you are a seasoned pro or someone just starting out, you know how much of a hassle summer and warm weather can be. In the summer, all the elements are against you, and making cake pops can be quite challenging. Not only do you have to deal with the high temperatures, you also have to deal with humidity and dry heat, which will completely alter the consistency of the chocolate you are using.

Some types of chocolate will fare better in heat and humidity. Almond barks will melt the same way as they did during the cooler months. Since they are sold in a thick bar form, the heat has less exposed surface area through which to soften the chocolate. However, due to candy melts' shape and size, it takes a lot less time for the heat to soften the chips. If you touch one during the summer it will be soft and will bend instead of snapping when you try to break it in half. Candy melts do not fare well in summer heat, so many stores will stop carrying them from June to October.

If you don't treat the chocolate it will melt down into a thick, paste-like texture. To fix that and return it to normal consistency you will have to firm up the chocolate and restore its snap. To do so, place it in the freezer for a few minutes until it is hard again and breaks with a clean, smooth snap in half. Make sure to melt it right away before it has the chance to soften again. If it sweats, then the chocolate will seize, or turn into a lumpy consistency, and be ruined.

The other issue with summer heat is the time it takes to harden the chocolate. The pops will lose the glossy shine that they have from being freshly dipped and go into the normal matte finish without hardening. If you live in an area where it is hot during the day and cold at night, the best time to dip your pops would be at night so the cold air can harden the pops. If it is hot both day and night, you have two options. Dip your pops in an air-conditioned room or, after dipping, place them in the fridge to harden and set. However, taking them to the fridge after being dipped can cause the chocolate to bloom. Bloomed chocolate is purely a cosmetic issue and does not affect flavor.

The heat will also affect the finish that your pops will have. Since it takes so long for the pops to set in heat, you will end up with a finish that looks more like leather and that may also spot. Spotting occurs when internal air bubbles collapse and form small, dark-colored indentations. Spotting is most common if pops are left out in warm weather for a long period of time. Store the pops in the fridge or a cold environment to prevent this.

Yellow Sticks • • • • • • • • • • • • • • • • •

When making cake pops, you might find that some of the sticks begin to change color and become yellow shortly after being dipped. This is purely a cosmetic issue, not a sign that the pops have spoiled. The yellowing is the result of the moisture from the fat being absorbed into the paper of the sticks. This does not always happen but will occasionally, depending on the heat as well as on the type of cake and frosting combo used.

The yellowing has a greater likelihood of happening if the cake is from a boxed mix. Not only do most boxed cakes have a higher moisture content, but they also most have a higher fat content than homemade cakes, which tend to be drier and butter based. It is always best to seek out a butter-based recipe or replace the fat in the cake with applesauce to prevent this.

The type of frosting you use is just as important as the type of cake that goes into your pops. If you are using a cream cheese frosting or a butter cream high in fat, it is only a matter of time before the sticks change color. Most homemade frostings require a lot of butter, and when left out in the

heat they tend to separate, which allows the fat to seep into the lollipop sticks. To limit the yellowing of sticks, always try to pair a homemade cake with a canned frosting, which will limit the amount of fat and prolong the pops' freshness.

If you have been making pops for a long time and just noticed this happening lately, keep the season in mind. The warmer the weather, the more likely and faster the yellowing will occur due to the fat being at a warmer, liquid state. There are two main ways to slow down or prevent this from happening. After you have finished decorating your pops, individually wrap them and place them in the fridge to make the fat stay in a solid form.

The other method to prevent this completely is pre-dipping all the sticks into melted chocolate before making the pops. Let the chocolate harden, then once again dip the stick into melted chocolate and then your pops. This creates a barrier between the stick and cake that doesn't allow oil or fat to be absorbed into the stick. You could also use plastic sticks, but they are harder to find in stores and often require special online purchases. Another way to hide the yellowing is to dip the pop further into the chocolate so that it is not visible.

There are going to be times while creating pops that you will notice them oozing a clear yellow liquid. That liquid is nothing more than the fat that hasn't been absorbed into the stick trying to escape. What happens is the pressure from the inside causes the fat to seep out of any tiny exposed holes. It will always come out from the weak spots in the chocolate, anywhere there is an air bubble.

To prevent this, try not to stir the chocolate as much, and if you find yourself with a lot of air bubbles, you can gently shake them out. If needed, straining your chocolate through a metal sieve will also remove the air bubbles. Air bubbles are often found in thicker chocolate. If you add some oil and stir, most air bubbles will disappear. When tapping off the excess chocolate, pop air bubbles ahead of time.

You can always double dip the pops to prevent air bubbles from forming. If you find yourself with a pop that has started to leak oil, just set it aside and wait until this stops. Eventually the internal pressure will be relieved and the fat will stop coming out. Wipe the grease and cover the hole with melted chocolate. Remove the excess and set aside to dry.

Shipping Cake Pops •••••••

One of the greatest things about cake pops is sharing them with friends and loved ones. Sometimes in order to share them they need to be shipped, which can seem frightening considering the amount of work that went into them and how delicate cake pops are.

There are two main concerns with shipping: the pops can get crushed or crack, or they can melt during transit. Since you have no control over how the package is handled, you need to properly prepare them for shipping. It's a good idea not to use fragile components when decorating the pops since they might break off in transit. If you use sprinkles or fondant, attach them while the pop is still wet so it is more secure. If possible, try to make most of the designs with chocolate.

The key to a successful shipment is securing the pops in the package. There are two main ways to prevent them from moving. The first method involves bubble wrap. You can line the shipping box with bubble wrap and then individually wrap each cake pop in two layers of bubble wrap. Place them in the box in a single layer and stuff

the wrap in any gaps and on top. Stack another layer of pops if needed and add enough bubble wrap so that the pops do not move when the box is sealed shut. Before you tape the box, close the lid and give the package a good shake. When you shake the box you should not hear any noise or feel movement. If the pops are moving, you'll have to repack them. Any movement will put the pops at risk for damage during shipping.

The other and safer option is the double box method, which involves packing the pops in smaller boxes before being packed in the shipping box. The best size box to use is one that is approximately 8⅝″ × 5⅜″ × 1⅝″. A box that size can hold 6–8 round cake pops that were weighed to one-ounce portions before being dipped. Although it is not needed, if you wish line the smaller boxes with bubble wrap before filling with pops. After they are in the box, there will be a space in the center and the side of the box where the sticks all meet, and in those sections layer up more bubble wrap so the sticks don't move during transit. Close the boxes and give them a shake to hear if the pops move. If they don't move pack them into your shipping box. If you can't find a box that is approximately 8⅝″ × 5⅜″ × 1⅝″ you can also use stationary boxes that measure 10″ × 7″ × 2″, which can hold about a dozen cake pops.

When you ship the pops, ideally you want to pick a method of shipping that takes 2–3 days, as anything longer and the pops pose the risk of being damaged in transit. The less time they spend in transit the better. Another big concern with shipping is whether the pops will melt during transit. In the United States you can safely ship the pops without the use of ice packs from October thru May. June thru September is generally far too warm for shipping. It is best to avoid shipping if possible during those months. If you must ship, have pops shipped overnight. You will need to ship your pops with ice packs and will need to insulate your shipping box. To insulate your shipping box, cut half-inch-thick Styrofoam sheets to cover the base, walls, and top of the box, essentially creating another box made out of Styrofoam. Then pack the pops as you normally would and add an ice pack. You could also pack the pops inside of an insulated bag to help keep the pops as cold as possible.

Preparing the Cake

Almond Cake • • • • • • • • • • • • • • •

Yield: Approximately 14 ounces

Ingredients

- 1½ cups flour
- 1 teaspoon baking powder
- ½ cup butter, room temperature
- ¾ cup white sugar
- 3 eggs, room temperature
- 1 tablespoon almond extract
- ¼ cup milk
- ½ cup finely chopped almonds

1. Preheat oven to 350°F (175°C). Grease and flour a 9 × 9 inch cake pan.

2. Sift together the flour and baking powder. Set aside.

3. In a large bowl, cream together the butter and sugar until combined. Beat in the eggs one at a time and almond extract until combined.

4. Add the flour mixture and alternate with the milk, mixing until combined, scraping down the sides if needed.

5. Mix in the chopped almonds.

6. Bake in the preheated oven for twenty to thirty minutes, or until top springs back when lightly touched.

7. Allow to fully cool before crumbling for cake balls.

Banana Cake • • • • • • • • • • • • • • •

Yield: Approximately 17 ounces

Ingredients

- ¾ cup flour
- ½ teaspoon of cinnamon
- ½ teaspoon baking soda
- 5 tablespoons butter, room temperature
- ¾ cup white sugar
- 1 egg, room temperature
- ¾ cup of mashed ripe bananas
- 1 teaspoon vanilla
- ¼ cup milk

1. Preheat oven to 350°F (175°C). Grease and flour a 9 × 9 inch cake pan.

2. Sift together the flour, baking soda, and cinnamon. Set aside.

3. In a large bowl, cream together the butter and sugar. Beat in the egg and vanilla until combined, then beat in the mashed bananas.

4. Add the flour mixture, scraping down the sides if needed, and mix until combined.

5. Add the milk and beat until smooth. Pour the batter into the prepared pan.

6. Bake in the preheated oven for twenty to thirty minutes, or until top springs back when lightly touched.

7. Allow to fully cool before crumbling for cake balls.

Carrot Cake • • • • • • • • • • • • • •

Yield: Approximately 20 ounces

Ingredients

- 1 cup flour
- 1 teaspoon cinnamon
- ⅛ teaspoon nutmeg
- 1 teaspoon baking soda
- 1 teaspoon baking powder
- ½ cup butter, room temperature
- ¾ cup white sugar
- 2 eggs, room temperature
- 1 teaspoon vanilla
- 1½ cups finely grated carrots

1. Preheat oven to 350°F (175°C). Grease and flour a 9 × 9 inch cake pan.

2. Sift together the flour, cinnamon, nutmeg, baking soda, and baking powder. Set aside.

3. In a large bowl, cream together the butter and sugar until combined. Beat in the eggs one at a time until combined, then beat in the vanilla.

4. Add the flour mixture and mix until combined, scraping down the sides if needed.

5. Mix in the finely grated carrots.

6. Bake in the preheated oven for twenty to thirty minutes, or until top springs back when lightly touched.

7. Allow to fully cool before crumbling for cake balls.

Chocolate Cake •••••••••

Yield: Approximately 27 ounces

Ingredients

- 1¾ cups flour
- 1 teaspoon baking soda
- ¼ teaspoon baking powder
- ½ cup cocoa powder
- ½ cup butter, room temperature
- 1 cup white sugar
- 2 eggs, room temperature
- 1 teaspoon vanilla
- ¾ cup strongly brewed coffee

1. Preheat oven to 350°F (175°C). Grease and flour a 9 × 13 inch cake pan.

2. Sift together the flour, baking soda, and baking powder. Set aside.

3. In a large bowl, cream together the butter and sugar until combined. Beat in the cocoa powder, the eggs one at a time until combined, then beat in the vanilla.

4. Alternate adding the flour mixture and strongly brewed coffee, scraping down the sides if needed, and mix until combined.

5. Bake in the preheated oven for twenty to thirty minutes, or until top springs back when lightly touched.

6. Allow to fully cool before crumbling for cake balls.

Coconut Cake ● ● ● ● ● ● ● ● ● ● ● ●

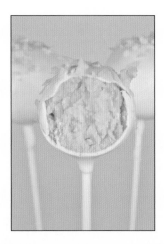

Yield: Approximately 14 ounces

Ingredients

- 1 cup flour
- 1 teaspoon baking powder
- ½ cup butter, room temperature
- ½ cup white sugar
- 2 eggs, room temperature
- 1 tablespoon coconut extract
- ¼ cup coconut milk
- ¼ cup shredded coconut

1. Preheat oven to 350°F (175°C). Grease and flour a 9 × 9 inch cake pan.

2. Sift together the flour and baking powder. Set aside.

3. In a large bowl, cream together the butter and sugar until combined. Beat in the eggs one at a time and coconut extract until combined.

4. Add the flour mixture and alternate with the coconut milk, mixing until combined, scraping down the sides if needed.

5. Mix in the shredded coconut.

6. Bake in the preheated oven for twenty to thirty minutes, or until top springs back when lightly touched.

7. Allow to fully cool before crumbling for cake balls.

Cookies and Cream Cake

Yield: Approximately 16 ounces

Ingredients

- 1 cup flour
- 1 teaspoon baking powder
- ½ cup butter, room temperature
- ¾ cup white sugar
- 2 eggs, room temperature
- 1 teaspoon vanilla
- ¼ cup milk
- ¾ cup of crushed Oreo cookies

1. Preheat oven to 350°F (175°C). Grease and flour a 9 × 9 inch cake pan.

2. Sift together the flour and baking powder. Set aside.

3. In a large bowl, cream together the butter and sugar until combined. Beat in the eggs one at a time until combined, then beat in the vanilla.

4. Add the flour mixture and alternate with the milk, mixing until combined, scraping down the sides if needed.

5. Mix in the Oreo cookies.

6. Bake in the preheated oven for twenty to thirty minutes, or until top springs back when lightly touched.

7. Allow to fully cool before crumbling for cake balls.

Lemon Cake ● ● ● ● ● ● ● ● ● ● ● ● ● ● ● ●

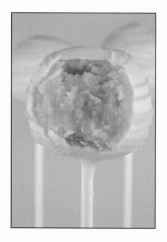

Yield: Approximately 18 ounces

Ingredients

- 1 cup flour
- 1 teaspoon baking powder
- ½ cup of butter, room temperature
- ¾ cup white sugar
- 2 eggs, room temperature
- 1 teaspoon vanilla
- 1½ teaspoons finely grated lemon zest
- ½ cup fresh-squeezed lemon juice

1. Preheat oven to 350°F (175°C). Grease and flour a 9 × 9 inch cake pan.

2. Sift together the flour and baking powder. Set aside.

3. In a large bowl, cream together the butter and sugar until combined. Beat in the eggs one at a time until combined, then beat in the vanilla and lemon zest.

4. Alternate adding the flour mixture and lemon juice, scraping down the sides if needed, and mix until combined.

5. Bake in the preheated oven for twenty to thirty minutes, or until top springs back when lightly touched.

6. Allow to fully cool before crumbling for cake balls.

Note

If you prefer a more subtle lemon flavor, replace half of the lemon juice with water.

Peanut Butter Cake • • • • • • •

Yield: Approximately 21 ounces

Ingredients

* 1 cup flour
* 1 teaspoon baking powder
* ½ cup butter, room temperature
* ½ cup peanut butter
* 1 cup white sugar
* 2 eggs, room temperature
* 1 teaspoon vanilla
* ⅓ cup milk
* ¼ cup finely chopped peanuts

1. Preheat oven to 350°F (175°C). Grease and flour a 9 × 9 inch cake pan.

2. Sift together the flour and baking powder. Set aside.

3. In a large bowl, cream together the butter, peanut butter, and sugar until combined. Beat in the eggs one at a time until combined, then beat in the vanilla.

4. Add the flour mixture and alternate with the milk, mixing until combined, scraping down the sides if needed.

5. Mix in the peanuts.

6. Bake in the preheated oven for twenty to thirty minutes, or until top springs back when lightly touched.

7. Allow to fully cool before crumbling for cake balls.

Strawberry Cake • • • • • • • • • • •

Yield: Approximately 30 ounces

Ingredients

- 1½ cups flour
- 1 teaspoon baking powder
- 3-ounce package of strawberry-flavored gelatin
- ¾ cup of butter, room temperature
- 1¼ cups white sugar
- 2 eggs, room temperature
- 1 teaspoon vanilla
- 1¼ cups of strawberry puree made from frozen strawberries

1. Preheat oven to 350°F (175°C). Grease and flour a 9 × 13 inch cake pan.

2. Sift together the flour, baking soda, and gelatin. Set aside.

3. In a large bowl, cream together the butter and sugar. Beat in the eggs one at a time until combined, then beat in the vanilla.

4. Alternate adding the flour mixture with strawberry puree, scraping down the sides if needed, and mix until combined.

5. Bake in the preheated oven for twenty to thirty minutes, or until top springs back when lightly touched.

6. Allow to fully cool before crumbling for cake balls.

Yellow Cake • • • • • • • • • • • • • • •

Yield: Approximately 27 ounces

Ingredients

- 1¾ cups flour
- 1½ teaspoons baking powder
- ¾ cup butter, chilled
- 1½ cups white sugar
- 8 egg yolks, chilled
- 1 teaspoon vanilla
- ½ cup milk, chilled

1. Preheat oven to 350°F (175°C). Grease and flour a 9 × 13 inch cake pan.

2. Sift together the flour and baking powder to remove any lumps. Set aside.

3. In a large bowl, cream together the butter and sugar. Add the egg yolks one at a time to the butter and sugar mixture, stir in the vanilla, and beat until combined.

4. Add the flour mixture in thirds, alternating with two additions of milk, mixing just until combined. You will start and finish with the flour. Pour the batter into the prepared pan.

5. Bake in the preheated oven for twenty-five to thirty minutes, or until top springs back when lightly touched.

6. Allow to fully cool before crumbling for cake balls.

Butter Cream Frosting • • • • • • • • • • • • • • • • • • •

Yield: Approximately 18 ounces

Ingredients

- 1 cup butter, softened
- 3 cups powdered sugar, sifted
- 1 tablespoon vanilla extract

1. Sift the powdered sugar through a metal sieve to remove any lumps.

2. Cream the butter in a stand mixer with a paddle attachment for a few minutes on the lowest setting until slightly whipped.

3. Add the powdered sugar one cup at a time until fully blended.

4. Mix in the vanilla extract and beat on medium-high speed for three minutes until fluffy.

Note

Add another cup of powdered sugar for a thicker consistency frosting and a sweeter taste.

Variation

For chocolate butter cream, mix in ½ cup of cocoa powder.

Cream Cheese Frosting •

Yield: Approximately 20 ounces

Ingredients

- 4 ounces butter, softened
- 4 ounces cream cheese, softened
- 3 cups powdered sugar
- 1 teaspoon vanilla extract

1. Sift the powdered sugar through a metal sieve to remove any lumps.

2. Cream the butter and cream cheese in a stand mixer with a paddle attachment on the lowest setting for a few minutes until slightly whipped.

3. Add the powdered sugar one cup at a time until fully blended.

4. Mix in the vanilla extract and beat on medium-high speed for three minutes until fluffy.

Note

Add another cup of powdered sugar for a thicker consistency frosting. For a more intense cream cheese flavor, increase the amount of cream cheese used. Any cake pops made with cream cheese frosting will require refrigeration.

Marshmallow Fondant • • • • • • • • • • • • • • • •

Ingredients

- 1 pound white mini-marshmallows
- 2 tablespoons water
- 2 pounds powdered sugar
- ½ cup shortening

1. Grease a microwave-safe bowl with the shortening and melt the marshmallows with two tablespoons of water in the microwave. Microwave in thirty-second intervals, stirring after each until fully melted.

2. Grease the bowl of a stand mixer as well as the dough hook attachment with shortening.

3. Sift three-quarters of the powdered sugar into the bowl and add the marshmallow mixture. Mix on low speed until it starts to come together.

4. Once it starts to pull away from the sides, generously grease your hands as well as a countertop with the shortening and knead the remaining quarter of sugar into mixture. Knead until it is smooth and pliable.

Royal Icing • • • • • • • • • • • • • • •

Ingredients

- 2 egg whites
- 2 pounds powdered sugar
- 2 teaspoons lemon juice

1. In a stand mixer, fitted with a whisk attachment, beat the egg whites and lemon juice on medium speed.

2. Slowly add powdered sugar a little at a time until it is fully combined. Keep adding the sugar until it resembles a thick frosting and forms a peak when the whisk is removed. Not all of the powdered sugar will be used. To create a stiff consistency icing, keep adding powdered sugar a spoonful at a time until it is thick and forms firm peaks. To thin down the icing, add a teaspoon of water until the icing is fluid.

Seven-minute Frosting • • • • • • • • • • • • • • • •

Yield: Approximately 10 ounces

Ingredients

- ¾ cup sugar
- 1 tablespoon light corn syrup
- 3 large egg whites
- 1 teaspoon vanilla extract

1. In a heatproof glass bowl, whisk together all the ingredients over a pot of simmering water. Make sure the water does not touch the bottom of the bowl.

2. Whisk the ingredients together until the sugar has dissolved and the mixture is warm to the touch. You should not feel any sugar granules between your fingers.

3. Once the sugar has dissolved, using a handheld mixer, beat the mixture on high for five to seven minutes until light and fluffy.

Whipped Ganache • • • • • • • • •

Yield: Approximately 18 ounces

Ingredients

- 8 ounces of semisweet or bittersweet chocolate
- 1 cup heavy cream
- ⅛ teaspoon coarse salt

1. Coarsely chop the chocolate using a serrated knife.

2. Bring the cream to a boil over medium-high heat. Pour the cream over the chocolate, add salt, and allow to sit for ten minutes before stirring.

3. Stir with a whisk until smooth and shiny. Allow to cool to room temperature, stirring often.

4. Beat in a stand mixer on medium-high speed for two to four minutes until fluffy and light in color.

Note

Because of the cream in this recipe, cake pops using ganache as the binder will require refrigeration.

Basic Cake Pops • • • • • • • • • • • •

Supplies

- Cake filling of your choice
- White candy melts
- Pastel nonpareil sprinkles

Tools

- Digital scale
- Sheet pan
- Microwave-safe bowls
- Lollipop sticks

1. Hand weigh the cake into one-ounce portions. Roll them into balls and set aside on a sheet pan. Place in the fridge while you prepare the candy melts.

2. Melt the white candy melts according to the directions on the package.

3. Remove the cake from the fridge. Dip each stick into the candy melts and insert it halfway into each cake pop.

4. Once the candy melts have fully set and the cake is back at room temperature, the pops are ready to be dipped. Fully submerge the pops into the white candy melts and tap off any excess.

5. While still wet, cover the entire pop with sprinkles. Allow to fully set.

Animal Prints

Giraffe Print Cake Pops • • • •

Supplies

- Cake filling of your choice
- Yellow candy melts
- Brown petal dust
- Confectioner's glaze
- Flavorless vodka or extract

Tools

- Digital scale
- Sheet pan
- Microwave-safe bowls
- Lollipop sticks
- Soft-bristle paintbrushes

1. Begin by hand weighing the cake into one-ounce portions. Roll them into balls and flatten the tops until you have rounded flat circles. Place them on a sheet pan in the refrigerator while you prepare the candy melts.

2. Melt the candy melts according to the directions on the package.

3. Remove the cake from the fridge. Dip each stick into the candy melts and insert it halfway into each cake pop. Once the candy melts have fully set and the cake is back at room temperature, you are ready to dip the pops. Fully submerge the pops into the candy melts and tap off any excess. Place in a stand and allow to set.

4. Create a 50/50 mixture with the confectioner's glaze and flavorless vodka or extract of your choosing. Add a drop at a time to the brown petal dust until a paint-able consistency is achieved.

5. Using a soft bristle brush, paint large blobs, leaving a small space between each one. Allow to dry.

Leopard Print Cake Pops •••••••••••••••••••

Supplies

- Cake filling of your choice
- Peanut butter candy melts
- Brown petal dust
- Black petal dust
- Confectioner's glaze
- Flavorless vodka or extract

Tools

- Digital scale
- Sheet pan
- Microwave-safe bowls
- Lollipop sticks
- Soft-bristle paintbrushes

1. Begin by hand weighing the cake into one-ounce portions. Roll them into a ball and flatten the top until you have a rounded flat circle. Place them on a sheet pan in the refrigerator while you prepare the candy melts.

2. Melt the candy melts according to the directions on the package.

3. Remove the cake from the fridge. Dip each stick into the candy melts and insert them halfway into each cake pop.

4. Once the candy melts have fully set and the cake is back at room temperature, you are ready to dip the pops. Fully submerge the pops into the candy melts and tap off any excess. Place in a stand and allow to set.

5. Create a 50/50 mixture with the confectioner's glaze and flavorless vodka or extract of your choosing. Add a drop at a time to the brown petal dust until a paintable consistency is achieved.

6. Using a soft-bristle brush, paint spots randomly on the pops and allow to dry. Once dry create a paintable mixture using the black petal dust and 50/50 mixture and paint short lines around the brown spots. Allow to dry.

Zebra Print Cake Pops • • • • • • • • • • • • • • •

Supplies

- Cake filling of your choice
- White candy melts
- Black petal dust
- Confectioner's glaze
- Flavorless vodka or extract

Tools

- Digital scale
- Sheet pan
- Microwave-safe bowls
- Lollipop sticks
- Soft-bristle paintbrushes

1. Begin by hand weighing the cake into one-ounce portions. Roll them into a ball and flatten the top until you have a rounded flat circle. Place them on a sheet pan in the refrigerator while you prepare the candy melts.

2. Melt the candy melts according to the directions on the package.

3. Remove the cake from the fridge. Dip each stick into the candy melts and insert them halfway into each cake pop.

4. Once the candy melts have fully set and the cake is back at room temperature, you are ready to dip the pops. Fully submerge the pops into the candy melts and tap off any excess. Place in a stand and allow to set.

5. Create a 50/50 mixture with the confectioner's glaze and flavorless vodka or extract of your choosing. Add a drop at a time to the black petal dust until a paintable consistency is achieved.

6. Paint a series of horizontal stripes onto the pop while slightly wiggling the paintbrush so the lines are not perfectly straight.

Arctic

Mountain Top
Cake Pops ● ● ● ● ● ● ● ● ● ● ● ● ● ● ●

Supplies

- Cake filling of your choice
- Gray candy melts
- White candy melts
- Silver luster dust

Tools

- Digital scale
- Sheet pan
- Microwave-safe bowls
- Lollipop sticks
- Plastic bag
- Soft-bristle paintbrush

1. Begin by hand weighing the cake into one-ounce portions. Roughly shape them into cones and use your fingers to create various indentations for a rocky effect. Place them on a sheet pan in the refrigerator while you prepare the candy melts.

2. Melt the gray candy melts according to the directions on the package.

3. Remove the cake from the fridge. Dip each stick into the candy melts and insert them halfway into each cake pop.

4. Once the candy melts have fully set and the cake is back at room temperature, you are ready to dip the pops. Fully submerge the pops into the candy melts and tap off any excess. Place in a stand and allow to set.

5. Using a soft-bristle paintbrush, lightly dust the pops with the silver luster dust.

6. Melt the white candy melts in a small plastic bag and snip off a corner. Pipe the white candy melts on the top of the pop and allow to spill over to create a snowy peak.

Penguin Cake Pops ● ● ● ● ● ● ●

Supplies

- Cake filling of your choice
- Black candy melts
- White candy melts
- Orange rainbow chips
- Orange star sprinkles

Tools

- Digital scale
- Sheet pan
- Microwave-safe bowls
- Lollipop sticks
- Plastic bags

1. Begin by hand weighing the cake into one-ounce portions. Roll them into ovals and flatten them slightly. Place them on a sheet pan in the refrigerator while you prepare the candy melts.

2. Melt the black candy melts according to the directions on the package. Remove the cake from the fridge. Dip each stick into the candy melts and insert them halfway into each cake pop.

3. Once the candy melts have fully set and the cake is back at room temperature, you are ready to dip the pops. Fully submerge the pops into the candy melts and tap off any excess. Place in a stand and allow to set.

4. Melt white and black candy melts in separate small plastic bags and snip off the corners. Using the white candy melts, outline the belly, fill it in, and tap to smooth out. Make sure you pipe the belly a smaller size than you want since it will expand when you tap the pop. While the belly is still wet, attach the star sprinkles for feet and the rainbow chip for the nose.

5. Dot on the eyes with the black candy melts.

Polar Bear Cake Pops ● ● ● ● ● ● ● ● ● ● ● ● ● ● ● ●

Supplies

- Cake filling of your choice
- White candy melts
- Black candy melts
- Pink candy melts
- Smarties

Tools

- Digital scale
- Sheet pan
- Microwave-safe bowls
- Lollipop sticks
- Plastic bags
- Soft-bristle paintbrush

1. Begin by hand weighing the cake into one-ounce portions. Roll them into balls and flatten them slightly. Place them on a sheet pan in the refrigerator while you prepare the candy melts.

2. Melt the white candy melts according to the directions on the package.

3. Remove the cake from the fridge. Dip each stick into the candy melts and insert them halfway into each cake pop. Dip the tips of two Smarties into the candy melts and attach at the top of the pop for ears.

4. Once the candy melts have fully set and the cake is back at room temperature, you are ready to dip the pops. Fully submerge the pops into the candy melts and tap off any excess. Place in a stand and allow to set.

5. Using a soft-bristle paintbrush, dab candy melts all over the cake pop to create the fur texture. Allow to set.

6. Melt white, pink, and black candy melts in separate small plastic bags and snip off the corners. Using the white candy melts, pipe the snout and eyebrows onto the pops. With the pink candy melts, pipe a dot in each ear and allow to set. Once the snout has set, pipe the eyes, nose, and mouth with black candy melts.

Walrus Cake Pops •••••••••

Supplies

- Cake filling of your choice
- Chocolate candy melts
- Peanut butter candy melts
- Black candy melts
- White candy melts

Tools

- Digital scale
- Sheet pan
- Microwave-safe bowls
- Lollipop sticks
- Plastic bags
- Soft-bristle paintbrush

1. Begin by hand weighing the cake into one-ounce portions. Roll them into balls and flatten the tops until you have flat circles. Place them on a sheet pan in the refrigerator while you prepare the candy melts.

2. Melt the chocolate candy melts according to the directions on the package.

3. Remove the cake from the fridge. Dip each stick into the candy melts and insert them halfway into each cake pop.

4. Once the candy melts have fully set and the cake is back at room temperature, you are ready to dip the pops. Fully submerge the pops into the candy melts and tap off any excess. Place in a stand and allow to set.

5. After the pops have set, use a soft-bristle paintbrush to dab on melted chocolate candy melts all over the surface to give the pop a textured finish.

6. Melt the white, black, and peanut butter candy melts in separate small plastic bags and snip off the corners. With the peanut butter candy melts, pipe on the cheeks and tap to smooth them out. Allow to set.

7. With the white candy melts, pipe on the tusks and allow to set. Lastly, pipe on the eyes, nose, and the dots onto the cheeks using the black candy melts.

Baby Shower

Baby in Blanket Cake Pops ● ● ● ● ● ● ● ● ● ● ● ● ● ●

Supplies

- Cake filling of your choice
- Pink candy melts
- Peanut butter candy melts
- White candy melts
- Yellow candy melts
- Black candy melts

Tools

- Digital scale
- Sheet pan
- Microwave-safe bowls
- Lollipop sticks
- Plastic bags

1. Hand weigh the cake into two separate portions for each pop—.90 of an ounce for the body and .40 of an ounce for the head—and roll them into balls. Place them on a sheet pan in the refrigerator for a few minutes while you prepare the candy melts.

2. Melt the pink candy melts according to the directions on the package. Remove the cake balls from the fridge. Dip the sticks into the candy melts and insert them through the larger cake balls so that a quarter of an inch of the sticks is exposed at the top. Dip the sticks once more into the melts and attach the small balls on top.

3. Once the candy melts have fully set and the cake is back at room temperature, the pops are ready to be dipped. Fully submerge the pops into the pink candy melts and tap off any excess. Allow them to set.

4. While the pops are drying, melt the peanut butter candy melts according to the directions on the package. Once the pops are dry, fill a spoon with the peanut butter candy melts and gently tap the upper ball into the spoon to create the face. Allow the excess to fall off, invert the cake pop, and gently shake side to side to smooth out the face, then set aside to dry.

5. Melt the black, white, pink, and yellow candy melts in separate small plastic bags, then snip the corners off. With the white candy melts, pipe a wavy line around the face going down the length of the body. Also draw dots with the white candy melts to create flowers. Using the yellow melts, pipe a dot in the center of the flowers and allow to dry.

6. Using the black candy melts, pipe a curl for the hair as well as a U for the eyes.

7. Using pink candy melts, pipe a small circle on the face for the base of the pacifier.

8. Allow to set, then pipe a smaller ring around the base created and add a dot on top of the pacifier. Allow to fully set.

Bear Cake Pops • • • • • • • • • • •

Supplies

- Cake filling of your choice
- Pink candy melts
- White candy melts
- Black candy melts
- Mini heart sprinkles
- Smarties

Tools

- Digital scale
- Sheet pan
- Microwave-safe bowls
- Lollipop sticks
- Plastic bags

1. Begin by hand weighing the cake into one-ounce portions. Roll them into balls and flatten the tops until you have flat circles. Place them on a sheet pan in the refrigerator while you prepare the candy melts.

2. Melt the pink candy melts according to the directions on the package.

3. Remove the cake from the fridge. Dip each stick into the candy melts and insert them halfway into each cake pop. Dip two Smarties into the melts and attach at the top of the cake for the ears.

4. Once the candy melts have fully set and the cake is back at room temperature, you are ready to dip the pops. Fully submerge the pops into the candy melts and tap off any excess. Place in a stand and allow to set.

5. Melt the white and black candy melts in separate small plastic bags and snip off the corners. Using the white candy melts, pipe a dot in each ear and an oval snout. Tap the pop gently to smooth out. Allow to set.

6. Once set, pipe two dots for the eyes and the mouth with the black candy melts. Attach a mini heart sprinkle for the nose while the mouth is still wet.

Bow Cake Pops •••••••••••••

Supplies

- Cake filling of your choice
- Light blue candy melts
- Light blue sanding sugar

Tools

- Digital scale
- Sheet pan
- Microwave-safe bowls
- Lollipop sticks
- Plastic bag
- 1¾-inch bone-shaped cookie cutter

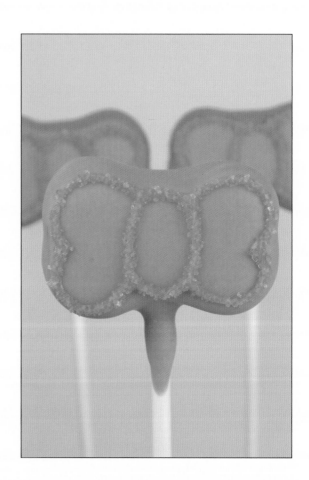

1. Stuff the cookie cutter with the cake mixture, using the palm of your hand to squeeze out any excess cake. Gently push the cake out of the cookie cutter. Chilling your dough ahead of time makes this process easier. Slightly flatten the cake to soften the edges. Place them on a sheet pan in the refrigerator while you prepare the candy melts.

2. Melt the light blue candy melts according to the directions on the package.

3. Remove the cake from the fridge. Dip each stick into the candy melts and insert them halfway into each cake pop.

4. Once the candy melts have fully set and the cake is back at room temperature, you are ready to dip the pops. Fully submerge the pops into the light blue candy melts and tap off any excess. Place in a stand and allow to set.

5. Melt the light blue candy melts in a small plastic bag and snip off a corner. Pipe the outline of the bow and, while still wet, sprinkle the sanding sugar on top. Allow to set.

Crying Baby Cake Pops ● ● ● ● ● ● ● ● ● ● ● ● ● ● ● ● ●

Supplies

- Cake filling of your choice
- Peanut butter candy melts
- Black candy melts
- Red candy melts
- White candy melts
- Blue candy melts
- Pink luster dust

Tools

- Digital scale
- Sheet pan
- Microwave-safe bowls
- Lollipop sticks
- Plastic bags
- Soft-bristle paintbrush

102

1. Begin by hand weighing the cake into one-ounce portions. Roll them into balls and set aside on a sheet pan. Place in the fridge while you prepare the candy melts.

2. Melt the peanut butter candy melts according to the directions on the package.

3. Remove the cake from the fridge. Dip each stick into the candy melts and insert them halfway into each cake pop.

4. Once the candy melts have fully set and the cake is back at room temperature, the pops are ready to be dipped. Fully submerge the pops into the peanut butter candy melts and tap off any excess. Allow to set. Once set, use the same candy melts to dot on a nose.

5. Melt the black, red, white, and blue candy melts in separate small plastic bags and snip off the corners. Using the black candy melts, pipe on the eyes, hair, and the large dot for the mouth. Allow to set.

6. Once the mouth has dried, pipe on a tooth with the white candy melts, a tongue with red candy melts, and tears with blue candy melts.

7. Once the candy melts have dried, lightly dust the cheeks with a soft-bristle paintbrush.

Diapered Baby Cake Pops ● ● ● ● ● ● ● ● ● ● ● ● ● ● ●

Supplies

- Cake filling of your choice
- White candy melts
- Peanut butter candy melts
- Black candy melts
- Blue candy melts
- Pink pearl dust

Tools

- Digital scale
- Sheet pan
- Microwave-safe bowls
- Lollipop sticks
- Plastic bags
- Soft-bristle paintbrush

1. Hand weigh the cake into two separate portions for each pop—.90 of an ounce for the body and .40 of an ounce for the head—and roll them into balls. Place them on a sheet pan in the refrigerator for a few minutes while you prepare the candy melts.

2. Melt the white candy melts according to the directions on the package. Remove the cake from the fridge. Dip the sticks into the white candy melts and insert each one fully through the larger cake ball, with a quarter of an inch of the stick being exposed at the top. Dip the sticks once more and attach the small balls on top.

3. Once the candy melts have fully set and the cake is back at room temperature, the pops are ready to be dipped. Fully submerge the pops into the white candy melts and tap off any excess. Allow them to set before proceeding.

4. While the pops are drying, melt the peanut butter candy melts according to the directions on the package. Once the pops are dry, dip them into the peanut butter melts three-quarters of the way up the pop, tap off the excess, and allow to dry.

5. Melt the black, white, and blue candy melts in separate plastic bags and snip off the corners. Pipe a line around the top of the diaper with the white melts and make swags below it. Allow to set.

6. Pipe a hair curl with black melts as well as two Us for the eyes.

7. Using blue candy melts, pipe a small circle on the face for the base of the pacifier. Allow to set, then pipe a smaller ring around the base created and add a dot to the top of the pacifier. Allow to fully set.

8. Lightly dust the cheeks with pink pearl dust using the soft-bristle paintbrush.

Gender Reveal Cake Pops •••••••••••••••••

Supplies

- Blue or pink cake filling
- White candy melts
- Black candy melts

Tools

- Digital scale
- Sheet pan
- Microwave-safe bowls
- Lollipop sticks
- Plastic bag

1. Begin by hand weighing the cake into one-ounce portions. Roll them into balls and set aside on a sheet pan. Place in the fridge while you prepare the candy melts.

2. Melt the white candy melts according to the directions on the package.

3. Remove the cake from the fridge. Dip each stick into the candy melts and insert them halfway into each cake pop.

4. Once the candy melts have fully set and the cake is back at room temperature, the pops are ready to be dipped. Fully submerge the pops into the white candy melts and tap off any excess. Allow to set.

5. Melt the black candy melts in a plastic bag and snip off a corner. Pipe question marks all over the pop.

Note

Make sure the white chocolate is not too thin so that the color of the cake doesn't show through the chocolate.

Variation

Instead of piping black question marks, you can pipe pink and blue over the pop.

Stacking Blocks Cake Pops • • • • • • • • • • • • • • • •

Supplies

- Cake filling of your choice
- Peanut butter candy melts
- Chocolate candy melts
- Red candy melts
- Red fondant

Tools

- Digital scale
- Sheet pan
- Microwave-safe bowls
- Lollipop sticks
- Plastic bags
- Pasta machine
- 1⅝-inch square-shaped cookie cutter
- ¾-inch numerical, letter, or teddy bear fondant cutter

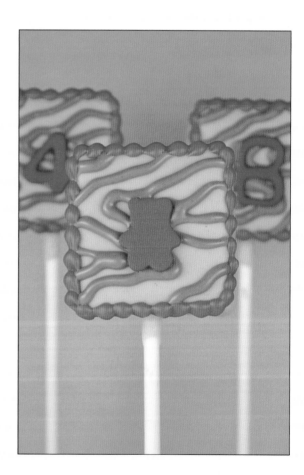

1. Stuff the cake mixture into each cookie cutter, using the palm of your hand to squeeze out any excess cake. Gently push the cake out of the cookie cutter. Chilling your dough ahead of time makes this process easier. Place the cake pops on a sheet pan in the refrigerator while you prepare the candy melts.

2. Melt the peanut butter and chocolate candy melts according to the directions on the package.

3. Remove the cake from the fridge. Dip each stick into the candy melts and insert them halfway into each cake pop.

4. Once the candy melts have fully set and the cake is back at room temperature, you are ready to dip the pops. Fully submerge the pops into the peanut butter candy melts and tap off any excess. Place in a stand and allow to set.

5. Roll out the fondant on the thickest setting and cut out various numbers, letters, and/or shapes.

6. Mix some chocolate candy melts into the peanut butter melts to darken the color. Place the candy melts into a small plastic bag and snip off the corner. Pipe a wood grain pattern on the surface of the pop and, while wet, attach a fondant cutout. Allow to set.

7. Melt the red candy melts in a small plastic bag and snip off a corner. Pipe a beaded border around the edge; using candy melts with a thicker consistency works best for this.

Teddy Bear
Cake Pops ● ● ● ● ● ● ● ● ● ● ● ● ● ● ● ● ●

Supplies

- Cake filling of your choice
- Chocolate candy melts
- Pink candy melts
- Black candy melts
- Jumbo pumpkin sprinkles

Tools

- Digital scale
- Sheet pan
- Microwave-safe bowls
- Lollipop sticks
- Plastic bags
- Soft-bristle paintbrush
- 2-inch gingerbread man–shaped cookie cutter

1. Stuff the cookie cutter with the cake mixture, using the palm of your hand to squeeze out any excess cake. Gently push the cake out of the cookie cutter. Chilling your dough ahead of time makes this process easier. Slightly flatten the cake to soften the edges. Place them on a sheet pan in the refrigerator while you prepare the candy melts.

2. Melt the chocolate candy melts according to the directions on the package.

3. Remove the cake from the fridge. Dip each stick into the candy melts and insert them halfway into each cake pop. Dip the pumpkin sprinkles into the candy melts and attach to the top of the head for the ears, stem side down.

4. Once the candy melts have fully set and the cake is back at room temperature, you are ready to dip the pops. Fully submerge the pops into the chocolate candy melts and tap off any excess. Place in a stand and allow to set.

5. Dab on candy melts all over the pop using a soft-bristle paintbrush to create texture on the pops.

6. Melt the pink and black candy melts in separate small plastic bags and snip off the corners. Using the pink candy melts, pipe on dots on the ears, paws, and the nose. While the nose is still wet, pipe a black dot on top.

Beach

Beach Ball Cake Pops ● ● ● ● ● ● ● ● ● ● ● ● ● ● ● ●

Supplies

- Cake filling of your choice
- White candy melts
- Red candy melts
- Yellow candy melts
- White sanding sugar
- Red sanding sugar
- Yellow sanding sugar
- Jumbo confetti sprinkles

Tools

- Digital scale
- Sheet pan
- Microwave-safe bowls
- Lollipop sticks
- Plastic bags
- Toothpick

1. Begin by hand weighing the cake into one-ounce portions. Roll them into balls and flatten the tops until you have flat circles. Place them on a sheet pan in the refrigerator while you prepare the candy melts.

2. Melt the white candy melts according to the directions on the package.

3. Remove the cake from the fridge. Dip each stick into the candy melts and insert them halfway into each cake pop.

4. Once the candy melts have fully set and the cake is back at room temperature, you are ready to dip the pops. Fully submerge the pops into the candy melts and tap off any excess. Place in a stand and allow to set.

5. With a toothpick, score the pop into six slightly curved panels.

6. Melt the white, yellow, and red candy melts in separate plastic bags and snip off the corners. Using the white candy melts, outline and fill in two of the panels scored earlier. While still wet, sprinkle sanding sugar over the candy melts and allow to set. Brush away any excess sugar and repeat the steps for the other colors. After all the colors have set, pipe a dot at the center and attach the jumbo confetti sprinkle.

Sandal Cake Pops • • • • • • • • • •

Supplies

- Cake filling of your choice
- White candy melts
- Pink candy melts
- Fondant

Tools

- Digital scale
- Sheet pan
- Microwave-safe bowls
- Lollipop sticks
- Plastic bags
- Pasta machine
- ½-inch flower plunger and impression mat

1. Begin by hand weighing the cake into one-ounce portions. Shape them to resemble a sandal and flatten the top of them. Place them on a sheet pan in the refrigerator while you prepare the candy melts and fondant.

2. Roll out the fondant on the thickest setting, using the plunger and impression mat to create a flower per pop. Set aside to dry.

3. Melt the candy melts according to the directions on the package. Place some of the pink melts in a plastic bag, cut the corner off and set aside.

4. Remove the cake from the fridge. Dip each stick into the white candy melts and insert them halfway into each cake pop. Once the candy melts have fully set and the cake is back at room temperature, you are ready to dip the pops. Fully submerge the pops into the white candy melts and tap off any excess. While wet, pipe dots of pink candy melts onto the pop then tap again until smooth. Allow to set.

5. Once set, pipe the beaded straps of the sandal and attach a flower in the middle, then pipe a dot of candy melts in the center of the flower.

Sand Castle
Cake Pops • • • • • • • • • • • • • • • •

Supplies

- Cake filling of your choice
- Peanut butter candy melts
- Red candy melts
- Cheerios
- Dry spaghetti

Tools

- Digital scale
- Sheet pan
- Microwave-safe bowls
- Lollipop sticks
- Plastic bags
- Food processor

1. Begin by hand weighing the cake into one-ounce portions. Shape them into cones and flatten the tops slightly. Using a lollipop stick make indentations on the top in the shape of an X. Place the cake balls on a sheet pan in the refrigerator while you prepare the candy melts.

2. Break the dried pasta into sections less than an inch long. Melt the red candy melts in a plastic bag, snip off the corner, and pipe a flag on top of each pasta string. Allow to set.

3. Crush the Cheerios in the food processor into fine grains.

4. Melt the peanut butter candy melts according to the directions on the package.

5. Remove the cake from the fridge. Dip each stick into the candy melts and insert them halfway into each cake pop.

6. Once the candy melts have fully set and the cake is back at room temperature, you are ready to dip the pops. Fully submerge the pops into the candy melts and tap off any excess. While still wet, sprinkle the entire pop with the crushed Cheerios and attach the flags to the top of the pops. Allow to set.

7. Using the peanut butter candy melts, pipe dots where the door will go, leaving space between each dot. While still wet, sprinkle the crushed Cheerios on top and allow to harden. When the candy melts have hardened, go back and add dots in the spaces between each dot and sprinkle with crushed Cheerios.

Sun Cake Pops • • • • • • • • • • • •

Supplies

- Cake filling of your choice
- Yellow candy melts
- Blue candy melts
- Black candy melts
- White chocolate chips

Tools

- Digital scale
- Sheet pan
- Microwave-safe bowls
- Lollipop sticks
- Plastic bags

1. Begin by hand weighing the cake into one-ounce portions. Roll them into balls and set aside on a sheet pan. Place in the fridge while you prepare the candy melts.

2. Melt the yellow candy melts according to the directions on the package.

3. Remove the cake from the fridge. Dip each stick into the candy melts and insert them halfway into each cake pop. With the candy melts, attach the white chocolate chips around the entire pop.

4. Once the candy melts have fully set and the cake is back at room temperature, you are ready to dip the pops. Fully submerge the pops into the candy melts and tap off any excess. Place in a stand and allow to set.

5. Melt the blue and black candy melts in small plastic bags and snip off the corners. Using the blue candy melts, pipe the outline of a pair of sunglasses and allow to set.

6. Once set, fill in the inside of the glasses by piping with black candy melts, and pipe a smile onto the face.

Note

When using a light color like yellow, remember to always use a light-colored cake as well. Otherwise, the cake will show through the candy melts.

Food

Baguette Cake Pops ● ● ● ● ● ● ● ● ● ● ● ● ● ● ● ● ●

Supplies

- Cake filling of your choice
- Peanut butter candy melts
- Brown petal dust

Tools

- Digital scale
- Sheet pan
- Microwave-safe bowls
- Lollipop sticks
- Soft-bristle paintbrush

1. Begin by hand weighing the cake into one-ounce portions. Roll them into elongated ovals. Using the edge of a knife or spoon, create three v-shaped indentations on one side of the cake. Place them on a sheet pan in the refrigerator for a few minutes while you prepare the candy melts.

2. Melt the peanut butter candy melts according to the directions on the package.

3. Remove the cake from the fridge. Dip each stick into the candy melts and insert them halfway into each cake pop.

4. Once the candy melts have fully set and the cake is back at room temperature, you are ready to dip the pops. Fully submerge the pops into the candy melts and tap off any excess. Place in a stand and allow to set.

5. Once the pops are dry, lightly dry dust them with brown petal dust to achieve a golden brown color.

Banana Cake Pops • • • • • • • • • •

Supplies

- Cake filling of your choice
- Yellow candy melts
- Chocolate candy melts

Tools

- Digital scale
- Sheet pan
- Microwave-safe bowls
- Lollipop sticks
- Plastic bag
- Toothpick
- Paper towel

1. Begin by hand weighing the cake into one-ounce portions. Shape them into mini bananas. Place them on a sheet pan in the refrigerator while you prepare the candy melts.

2. Melt the yellow and chocolate candy melts according to the directions on the package.

3. Remove the cake from the fridge. Dip the sticks into the candy melts and insert them halfway into each cake pop through the middle of the back.

4. Once the candy melts have fully set and the cake is back at room temperature, the pops are ready to be dipped. Fully submerge the pops into the yellow candy melts and tap off any excess. Allow to set.

5. With a toothpick, apply chocolate candy melts to the tips of the banana. While still wet, drag the toothpick through the chocolate to create four points on each tip. Apply dots of chocolate randomly over the entire pop and gently smear them with a paper towel or napkin to create a bruised banana.

Chocolate Chip Muffin Cake Pops •••••••••

Supplies

- Cake filling of your choice
- Peanut butter candy melts
- Mini chocolate chips
- Brown petal dust

Tools

- Digital scale
- Sheet pan
- Microwave-safe bowls
- Lollipop sticks
- Soft-bristle paintbrush
- 1¼ × ¾ inch daisy-shaped cookie cutter

1. Begin by hand weighing the cake into one-ounce portions. Roll them into logs wide enough to fit through the cookie cutter. Insert the cake through the cookie cutter, flattening the top and bottom so that it fills out the bottom creating a muffin shape. Place in the fridge while you prepare the candy melts.

2. Melt the peanut butter candy melts according to the directions on the package.

3. Remove the cake from the fridge. Dip each stick into the candy melts and insert them halfway into each cake pop.

4. Once the candy melts have fully set and the cake is back at room temperature, the pops are ready to be dipped. Fully submerge the pops into the candy melts and tap off any excess. While still wet, sprinkle mini chocolate chips on top. Allow to set.

5. Dry dust the pops with brown petal dust so the muffins look baked.

Corn Dog
Cake Pops • • • • • • • • • • • • • •

Supplies

- Cake filling of your choice
- Peanut butter candy melts
- Yellow candy melts
- Brown petal dust

Tools

- Digital scale
- Sheet pan
- Microwave-safe bowls
- Lollipop sticks
- Plastic bag
- Soft-bristle paintbrush

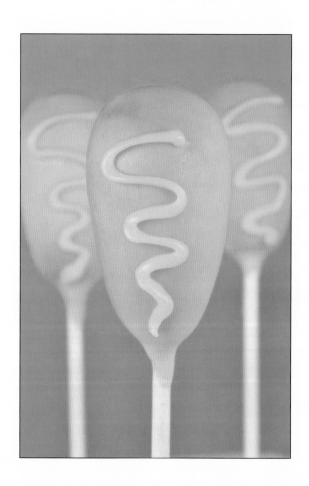

1. Begin by hand weighing the cake into one-ounce portions. Roll them to resemble a corn dog. Place them on a sheet pan in the refrigerator for a few minutes while you prepare the candy melts.

2. Melt the peanut butter candy melts according to the directions on the package.

3. Remove the cake from the fridge. Dip each stick into the candy melts and insert them halfway into each cake pop.

4. Once the candy melts have fully set and the cake is back at room temperature, you are ready to dip the pops. Fully submerge the pops into the candy melts and tap off any excess. Place in a stand and allow to set.

5. Once the pops are dry, lightly dry dust them with brown petal dust to achieve a golden brown color.

6. Melt the yellow candy melts in a plastic bag, snip off the corner, and pipe a wavy line going the length of the pop for mustard.

Doughnut Cake Pops

Supplies

- Cake filling of your choice
- Peanut butter candy melts
- Pink candy melts
- Nonpareils

Tools

- Digital scale
- Sheet pan
- Microwave-safe bowls
- Lollipop sticks
- Plastic bag
- Fondant ball tool

1. Begin by hand weighing the cake into one-ounce portions. Roll them into a ball and flatten the tops of them until you have a rounded, flat circle. Using the fondant ball tool create an indentation in the center of the cake. Place them on a sheet pan in the refrigerator while you prepare the candy melts.

2. Melt the candy melts according to the directions on the package.

3. Remove the cake from the fridge. Dip each stick into the candy melts and insert them halfway into each cake pop.

4. Once the candy melts have fully set and the cake is back at room temperature, you are ready to dip the pops. Fully submerge the pops into the candy melts and tap off any excess. Place in a stand and allow to set.

5. Melt the pink candy melts in a small plastic bag, snip off a corner, and pipe onto the doughnut. Allow it to slightly spill over the sides of the pop, and then sprinkle the nonpareils on top.

Egg Cake Pops •••••••••••••

Supplies

- Cake filling of your choice
- White candy melts
- Yellow candy melts
- Confectioner's glaze

Tools

- Digital scale
- Sheet pan
- Microwave-safe bowls
- Lollipop sticks
- Soft-bristle paintbrush

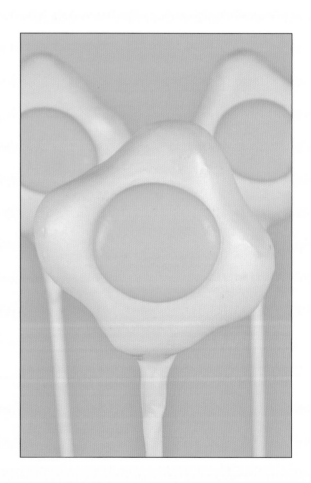

1. Begin by hand weighing the cake into one-ounce portions. Roll them into balls, flatten the tops, and shape them to resemble egg whites. Place them on a sheet pan in the refrigerator while you prepare the candy melts.

2. Melt the candy melts according to the directions on the package.

3. Remove the cake from the fridge. Dip each stick into the white candy melts and insert them halfway into each cake pop.

4. Once the candy melts have fully set and the cake is back at room temperature, the pops are ready to be dipped. Fully submerge the pops into the candy melts and tap off any excess. Allow to set.

5. Prepare the yellow candy melts in a plastic bag, snip off the corner, and pipe a circle in the center of the pop for the yolk. Allow to set.

6. Once the pops have set, paint the entire pop with confectioner's glaze to give the pop a glossy finish and allow to dry.

French Toast
Cake Pops

Supplies

- Cake filling of your choice
- Peanut butter candy melts
- Chocolate candy melts
- Yellow candy melts
- Brown petal dust

Tools

- Digital scale
- Sheet pan
- Microwave-safe bowls
- Lollipop sticks
- Plastic bags
- Soft-bristle paintbrush

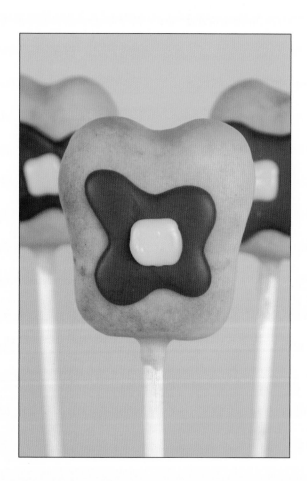

1. Begin by hand weighing the cake into one-ounce portions. Shape them to resemble slices of bread and set aside on a sheet pan. Place in the fridge while you prepare the candy melts.

2. Melt the peanut butter candy melts according to the directions on the package.

3. Remove the cake from the fridge. Dip each stick into the candy melts and insert them halfway into each cake pop.

4. Once the candy melts have fully set and the cake is back at room temperature, the pops are ready to be dipped. Fully submerge the pops into the candy melts and tap off any excess. Allow to set.

5. Once set, dry dust the entire pop with brown petal dust using a soft-bristle paintbrush.

6. Prepare the chocolate and yellow candy melts in separate plastic bags. Snip off a corner from each bag. Using the chocolate melts, pipe on the syrup and allow to set. Then, pipe a square on top of the syrup using the yellow melts for the butter.

Meatball Cake Pops • • • • • • •

Supplies

- Cake filling of your choice
- Chocolate candy melts
- Red candy melts
- White candy melts
- Yellow candy melts

Tools

- Digital scale
- Sheet pan
- Microwave-safe bowls
- Lollipop sticks
- Plastic bags
- Soft-bristle paintbrush
- Grater

1. Begin by hand weighing the cake into one-ounce portions. Roll them into balls and set aside on a sheet pan. Place in the fridge while you prepare the candy melts.

2. Melt the chocolate candy melts according to the directions on the package.

3. Remove the cake from the fridge. Dip each stick into the candy melts and insert them halfway into each cake pop.

4. Once the candy melts have fully set and the cake is back at room temperature, you are ready to dip the pops. Fully submerge the pops into the candy melts and tap off any excess. Place in a stand and allow to set.

5. Using a soft-bristle paintbrush, dab chocolate candy melts all over the pop to create texture and allow to set.

6. Finely grate the white candy melts using a metal grater.

7. Melt the red and yellow candy melts in separate plastic bags and snip off the corners. Using the yellow candy melts, pipe the pasta around the base of the pop. Using a thicker consistency candy melt works best for this step.

8. Pipe a pool of red melts on top for sauce and sprinkle with the grated white candy melts for cheese while still wet.

Popcorn Cake Pops • • • • • • • •

Supplies

- Cake filling of your choice
- Yellow candy melts
- Orange petal dust
- Marshmallows

Tools

- Digital scale
- Sheet pan
- Microwave-safe bowls
- Lollipop sticks
- Soft-bristle paintbrush

1. Begin by hand weighing the cake into one-ounce portions. Roll them into balls and set aside on a sheet pan. Place in the fridge while you prepare the candy melts.

2. Melt the candy melts according to the directions on the package.

3. Remove the cake from the fridge. Dip each stick into the candy melts and insert them halfway into each cake pop.

4. Slightly rip the marshmallows in half without completely tearing them into two pieces and attach them around the base of the cake.

5. Once the candy melts have fully set and the cake is back at room temperature, the pops are ready to be dipped. Fully submerge the pops into the candy melts and tap off any excess. Allow to set.

6. Dry dust the pops with orange petal dust using the soft-bristle paintbrush.

Variation

Dip the pops in white candy melts and dry dust them with yellow for lightly buttered popcorn.

Watermelon Cake Pops • • • • • • • • • • • • • • •

Supplies

- Pink cake filling
- Mini chocolate chips
- White candy melts
- Light green candy melts
- Green food coloring
- Flavorless vodka or extract

Tools

- Digital scale
- Sheet pan
- Microwave-safe bowls
- Lollipop sticks
- Soft-bristle paintbrush

1. Mix mini chocolate chips into the pink cake filling. Hand weigh the cake into one-ounce portions, roll them into elongated balls, and set aside on a sheet pan. Place in the fridge while you prepare the candy melts.

2. Melt the white and light green candy melts according to the directions on the package.

3. Remove the cake from the fridge. Dip each stick into the candy melts and insert them halfway into each cake pop.

4. Once the candy melts have fully set and the cake is back at room temperature, the pops are ready to be dipped. Fully submerge the pops into the white candy melts and tap off any excess. Allow to set. When the white melts have set, dip the pops once again, this time in the light green melts, and allow to set.

5. Mix the green food coloring with vodka or extract and brush on stripes with the soft-bristle paintbrush.

Variation

By following these simple steps as a base, you can create a wide variety of fruit pops. Using yellow cake mixed with white chocolate chips and dipped in yellow candy melts, you can create lemon cake pops.

Forest

Beaver Cake Pops • • • • • • • • • •

Supplies

- Cake filling of your choice
- Chocolate candy melts
- Peanut butter candy melts
- White candy melts
- Black candy melts
- Smarties

Tools

- Digital scale
- Sheet pan
- Microwave-safe bowls
- Lollipop sticks
- Plastic bags

1. Begin by hand weighing the cake into one-ounce portions. Roll them into balls and set aside on a sheet pan. Place in the fridge while you prepare the candy melts.

2. Melt the chocolate candy melts according to the directions on the package.

3. Remove the cake from the fridge. Dip each stick into the candy melts and insert them halfway into each cake pop. Dip two Smarties into the melts and attach at the top of the cake for the ears.

4. Once the candy melts have fully set and the cake is back at room temperature, you are ready to dip the pops. Fully submerge the pops into the candy melts and tap off any excess. Place in a stand and allow to set.

5. Melt the peanut butter, chocolate, white, and black candy melts in small plastic bags and snip off the corners. Using the peanut butter candy melts, pipe a dot in each ear and two more dots on the face to create cheeks. Tap the pop gently to smooth out. Allow to set.

6. Pipe the nose, two dots for the eyes, and three smaller dots on each cheek using the black melts. Using the chocolate candy melts, pipe three strands of hair on top. Lastly, using the white candy melts, pipe on the teeth.

Beehive Cake Pops •••••••••

Supplies

- Cake filling of your choice
- Yellow candy melts
- Black candy melts
- Yellow fondant
- White confetti sprinkles

Tools

- Digital scale
- Sheet pan
- Microwave-safe bowls
- Lollipop sticks
- Plastic bag

1. Roll tiny pieces of yellow fondant into teardrops. Melt the black candy melts in a plastic bag and snip off the corner. Drizzle the candy melts onto the yellow fondant and attach two white confetti sprinkles to the sides while still wet and set aside. These are your bees.

2. For each beehive, the cake needs to be hand weighed into three portions: .60 ounces for the bottom tier, .30 ounces for the middle tier, and .10 ounces for the top tier. Roll them into balls and slightly flatten them. Stack them on top of each other and set aside on a sheet pan. Place in the fridge while you prepare the candy melts.

3. Melt the yellow candy melts according to the directions on the package.

4. Remove the cake from the fridge. Dip the sticks into the candy melts and insert them completely through the bottom two layers of cake and halfway through the top layer.

5. Once the candy melts have fully set and the cake is back at room temperature, the pops are ready to be dipped. Fully submerge the pops into the yellow candy melts and tap off any excess. While still wet, place the fondant bees on top.

6. Using the black candy melts, pipe a dot onto the front of the pop and dashes around the pop.

Fox Cake Pops • • • • • • • • • • •

Supplies

- Cake filling of your choice
- Orange candy melts
- White candy melts
- Black candy melts
- Candy corn

Tools

- Digital scale
- Sheet pan
- Microwave-safe bowls
- Lollipop sticks
- Plastic bags

1. Begin by hand weighing the cake into one-ounce portions. Roll them into ovals and flatten them. Place them on a sheet pan in the refrigerator while you prepare the candy melts.

2. Melt the orange candy melts according to the directions on the package.

3. Remove the cake from the fridge. Dip each stick into the candy melts and insert them halfway into each cake pop.

4. Cut off the wider bottom layer of the candy corn. Dip the candy corn into the candy melts and attach to the top of the pop for ears. Allow to set.

5. Once the candy melts have fully set and the cake is back at room temperature, you are ready to dip the pops. Fully submerge the pops into the candy melts and tap off any excess. Allow to set.

6. Melt the white and black candy melts in separate plastic bags and snip off the corners. Using the white candy melts, outline the face, fill it in, and tap off to smooth. Also pipe the inner ears and allow to set. Pipe on two eyes and a nose with the black melts.

Hedgehog Cake Pops ·······

Supplies

- Cake filling of your choice
- Chocolate candy melts
- Black candy melts
- Slivered almonds

Tools

- Digital scale
- Sheet pan
- Microwave-safe bowls
- Lollipop sticks
- Plastic bag
- Food processor

1. Hand weigh the cake into one-ounce portions and shape into pears. Place them on a sheet pan in the refrigerator while you prepare the candy melts.

2. In a food processor, finely chop the slivered almonds.

3. Melt the chocolate candy melts according to the directions on the package. Remove the cake from the fridge. Dip each stick into the candy melts and insert them halfway into each cake pop.

4. Once the candy melts have fully set and the cake is back at room temperature, you are ready to dip the pops. Fully submerge the pops into the candy melts and tap off any excess.

5. While still wet, dip the wider half of the pops in the crushed almonds and allow to set.

6. Melt the black candy melts in a small plastic bag and snip off a corner. Pipe on eyes and a nose.

Mouse Cake Pops • • • • • • • • • •

Supplies

- Cake filling of your choice
- Gray candy melts
- Pink candy melts
- Black candy melts
- Pink fondant

Tools

- Digital scale
- Sheet pan
- Microwave-safe bowls
- Lollipop sticks
- Plastic bags
- ¾-inch rose petal cutter
- Pasta machine
- Soft-bristle paintbrush

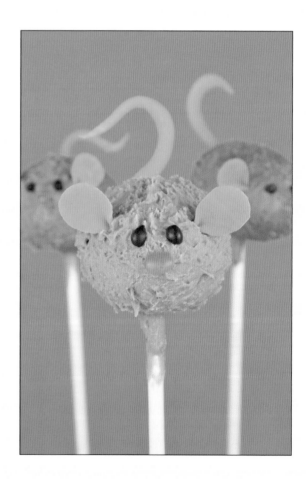

1. Roll out the fondant ahead of time on the thickest setting and cut out two petals for each pop with the rose petal cutter (these will be the ears). Pinch the pointed ends together and allow to fully harden. Also roll out tails and allow to harden.

2. Hand weigh the cake into one-ounce portions. Roll them into teardrops and set aside on a sheet pan. Place in the fridge while you prepare the candy melts.

3. Melt the gray candy melts according to the directions on the package.

4. Remove the cake from the fridge. Dip each stick into the candy melts and insert them halfway into each cake pop.

5. Once the candy melts have fully set and the cake is back at room temperature, the pops are ready to be dipped. Fully submerge the pops into the gray candy melts and tap off any excess. While still wet, insert the fondant ears and allow to set in a stand.

6. Dab the melted gray candy melts all over the pop with a soft-bristle paintbrush to create the fur texture. While still wet, attach the tail to the back of the pop.

7. Melt the pink and black candy melts in separate plastic bags and snip off the corners. Using the pink melts, pipe on the nose, and with the black melts, pipe on the eyes.

Mushroom Cake Pops••••••

Supplies

- Cake filling of your choice
- White candy melts
- Black candy melts
- Chocolate candy melts
- Brown petal dust

Tools

- Digital scale
- Sheet pan
- Microwave-safe bowls
- Lollipop sticks
- Stiff-bristle paintbrush
- Soft-bristle paintbrush
- Rounded tablespoon measure

1. Use a rounded tablespoon as a mold for the cap of the mushroom. Stuff the cake into the measuring spoon and gently remove. To create a stem, separate the cake into .40-ounce portions. Roll the balls into the shape of teardrops with flat tops instead of pointed tips. Place them on a sheet pan in the refrigerator while you prepare the candy melts.

2. Melt the white and black candy melts according to the directions on the package.

3. Remove the cake from the fridge. Using a stiff-bristle paintbrush, paint the black candy melts onto the flat side of the mushroom cap. Brush in even strokes all the way around the cap and in layers to create the texture of the gills. Dip the sticks into the white candy melts and insert them completely through the stems of the mushrooms, exposing the sticks.

4. Once the candy melts have fully set and your cake is back at room temperature, you are ready to dip the pops. Fully submerge the stem of the pop into the white candy melts and tap off any excess. Place the cap onto the stem and allow to set.

5. Melt the chocolate candy melts according to the directions on the package. Dip the caps of the pops in the melted chocolate so they slightly overlap the gills of the mushroom. Set back into the stand to dry.

6. When the caps have dried, lightly dust the stems with brown petal dust using the soft-bristle paintbrush.

Owl Cake Pops • • • • • • • • • • •

Supplies

- Cake filling of your choice
- Peanut butter candy melts
- Chocolate candy melts
- Rainbow chip sprinkles
- Orange, candy-coated sunflower seeds
- Orange star sprinkles
- Yellow confetti sprinkles
- Fondant

Tools

- Digital scale
- Sheet pan
- Microwave-safe bowls
- Lollipop sticks
- Plastic bags
- Toothpicks
- ⅝-inch circle fondant cutter
- Pasta machine

1. Begin by hand weighing the cake into one-ounce portions. Roll them into an oval shape and set them aside on a sheet pan. Place them in the fridge for a few minutes while you prepare the candy melts.

2. Melt the peanut butter candy melts according to the directions on the package.

3. Remove the cake from the fridge. Dip each stick into the candy melts and insert them halfway into each cake pop. Using candy melts, attach two rainbow chip sprinkles to the top of each of the pops for the ears.

4. Once the candy melts have fully set on the ears and where the stick was inserted, you are ready to dip the pops. Allow the pops to come to room temperature before dipping. Fully submerge the pops into the candy melts and tap off any excess. Place the pops into a stand and allow to fully dry.

5. While the pops are drying, melt the chocolate candy melts according to the directions on the package. Once the pops are dry, dip them again, in the chocolate candy melts, in a diagonal direction, covering both ears and creating a tan, triangular belly.

6. As the second coat of candy melts is drying, prepare the eyes. Roll out fondant on the thickest pasta machine setting and cut out circles. Set them aside until needed.

7. Take some of the peanut butter candy melts from earlier and place them in a small plastic bag. Snip off the corner of the bag and pipe a series of swags going across the tan portion of the pop on the belly. Allow to set.

8. Use a toothpick to dot on melted candy melts and attach the eyes just above the point of the tan triangle. Once set, attach yellow confetti sprinkles to the eyes and allow to set before you dot on melted black candy melts.

9. Between the eyes, add a dot of candy melts and glue on the candy-coated sunflower seed as the beak.

10. Attach the orange stars to the body of the owl for the feet.

Fun Designs

Balloon Cake Pops ● ● ● ● ● ● ● ●

Supplies

- Cake filling of your choice
- Candy melts of your choice
- White candy melts
- Jumbo heart sprinkles

Tools

- Digital scale
- Sheet pan
- Microwave-safe bowls
- Lollipop sticks
- Plastic bag

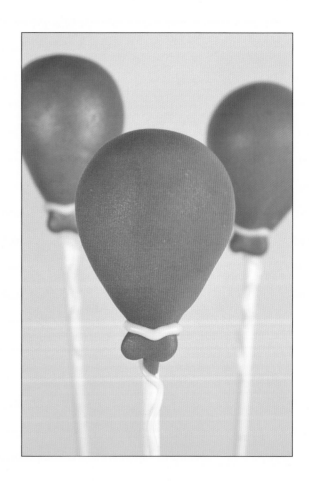

1. Hand weigh the cake into one-ounce portions and shape them into teardrops. Place in the fridge while you prepare the candy melts.

2. Melt the candy melts according to the directions on the package.

3. Remove the cake from the fridge. Dip the sticks into the candy melts and insert them halfway into the narrow ends of the cake balls.

4. Take a jumbo heart sprinkle and dip the pointed end into the candy melts. Insert it into the cake at the base, above the stick.

5. Once the candy melts have fully set and the cake is back at room temperature, you are ready to dip the pops. Fully submerge the pops into the candy melts and tap off any excess. Allow them to fully dry in a stand.

6. Melt the white candy melts in a small plastic bag, snip the corner off, and pipe on the string of the balloon.

Dynamite Cake Pops • • • • • • • •

Supplies

- Cake filling of your choice
- Red candy melts
- Fondant
- Black petal dust
- Red petal dust
- White petal dust

Tools

- Digital scale
- Sheet pan
- Microwave-safe bowls
- Lollipop sticks
- Soft-bristle paintbrush

1. Roll the fondant into a thin log and cut it into ¾-inch sections. Allow to fully harden before moving on.

2. Hand weigh the cake into one-ounce portions. Shape them into cylinders approximately 2½ inches long and set them aside on a sheet pan. Place in the fridge while you prepare the candy melts.

3. Melt the red candy melts according to the directions on the package.

4. Remove the cake from the fridge. Dip each stick into the candy melts and insert them halfway into each cake pop. If the cake gets distorted when the stick is inserted, roll it back and forth on a flat surface to smooth it out.

5. Once the candy melts have fully set and the cake is back at room temperature, you are ready to dip the pops. Fully submerge the pops into the candy melts and tap off any excess. Insert the fondant wicks created earlier into the top of each pop and allow them to fully dry in a stand.

6. After the pops have fully dried, tap the tips of the wick with a soft-bristle paintbrush using the petal dust. Start off with the black petal dust, then the red, and last, the white.

Flying Pig Cake Pops •••••••

Supplies

- Cake filling of your choice
- Pink candy melts
- Jumbo heart sprinkles
- Mini black confetti sprinkles
- Smarties
- Tic Tacs
- Fondant

Tools

- Digital scale
- Sheet pan
- Microwave-safe bowls
- Lollipop sticks
- Toothpick
- Pasta machine
- 1⅛-inch butterfly cutter

1. Ahead of time, roll out the fondant on the thickest setting of the pasta machine and cut out shapes with the butterfly cutter. Cut each butterfly in half to create individual wings and allow them to harden.

2. Once the wings have hardened, hand weigh the cake into one-ounce portions. Roll them into slightly elongated balls and place them in the fridge on a sheet pan for a few minutes while you prepare the candy melts.

3. Melt the pink candy melts according to the directions on the package.

4. Remove the cake from the fridge. Dip each stick into the candy melts and insert them halfway into each cake pop. Next, dip the round ends of the heart sprinkles into the melts and attach them to the tops of the cake balls for the ears.

5. Dip four Tic Tacs into the melts and attach them to the bottoms of the balls for the feet. For the noses, put a drop of the melts on the faces of the pigs and attach one Smartie per pig.

6. Once the candy melts have fully set and the cake is back at room temperature, you are ready to dip the pops. Fully submerge the pops into the candy melts and tap off any excess. Keep the faces of the pigs towards you as you tap off the excess.

7. While still wet, attach the wings created earlier to the tops of the pigs and allow the pops to fully dry.

8. Dip a toothpick into the melted pink candy melts and dot on the eyes. Attach the black confetti sprinkles and allow to set.

Gem Cake Pops •••••••••••••

Supplies

- Cake filling of your choice
- Candy melts of your choice
- Pearl dust of your choice
- Flavorless vodka or extract
- Confectioner's glaze

Tools

- Digital scale
- Sheet pan
- Microwave-safe bowls
- Lollipop sticks
- Soft-bristle paintbrush

1. Begin by hand weighing the cake into one-ounce portions. Roll them into balls and set aside on a sheet pan. Place in the fridge while you prepare the candy melts.

2. Melt the candy melts according to the directions on the package.

3. Remove the cake from the fridge. Dip each stick into the candy melts and insert them halfway into each cake pop.

4. Once the candy melts have fully set and the cake is back at room temperature, the pops are ready to be dipped. Fully submerge the pops into the candy melts and tap off any excess. Allow to set.

5. Once the pops have set, mix the flavorless vodka or extract with the pearl dust so it is a paintable consistency and paint the entire pop with it. It will take two to three coats to get an even layer and give the pops a metallic look.

6. When the pops have dried, using a soft-bristle paintbrush, paint on the confectioner's glaze, which will give the pops a wet, glossy look. The confectioner's glaze will take a few minutes to dry. Allow to fully dry before touching or bagging them.

Variation

For gem pops with a mirrored finished, use a soft-bristle paintbrush to wet the entire pop with water. Using a somewhat firm-bristle paintbrush, dip the tip into disco dust and press firmly on the pop while dabbing in a circular motion.

Magic Wand
Cake Pops • • • • • • • • • • • • • • •

Supplies

- Cake filling of your choice
- Black candy melts
- White candy melts

Tools

- Digital scale
- Sheet pan
- Microwave-safe bowls
- Lollipop sticks

1. Begin by hand weighing the cake into one-ounce portions. Shape them into cylinders approximately 2½ inches long and set them aside on a sheet pan. Place in the fridge while you prepare the candy melts.

2. Melt the black and white candy melts separately according to the directions on the package.

3. Remove the cake from the fridge. Dip each stick into the candy melts and insert them halfway into each cake pop. If the cake gets distorted when the stick is inserted, roll it back and forth on a flat surface to smooth it out.

4. Once the candy melts have fully set and the cake is back at room temperature, you are ready to dip the pops. Fully submerge the pops into the black candy melts and tap off any excess. Place the pops into a stand and allow them to fully dry.

5. After the pops have fully dried, slightly dip the tips of the wands into the white candy melts and allow to set.

Marbled Cake Pops · · · · · · · ·

Supplies

- Chocolate cake filling
- Vanilla cake filling
- Chocolate candy melts
- White candy melts

Tools

- Digital scale
- Sheet pan
- Microwave-safe bowls
- Lollipop sticks

1. Roll the chocolate and vanilla cakes together into one-ounce balls so the two flavors swirl. Place them on a sheet pan in the refrigerator while you prepare the candy melts.

2. Melt the chocolate and white candy melts according to the directions on the package.

3. Remove the cake from the fridge. Dip each stick into the candy melts and insert them halfway into each cake pop.

4. Once the candy melts have fully set and the cake is back at room temperature, you are ready to dip the pops.

5. To achieve the marble effect, drizzle white candy melts on top of the melted chocolate candy melts. Fully submerge the pops into the candy melts and rotate while pulling up. Tap off any excess while rotating. Add more white candy melts to the chocolate melts before dipping each pop. Place the pops into a stand and allow them to fully dry.

Paintbrush Tip Cake Pops · · · · · · · · · · · · · · · · ·

Supplies

- Cake filling of your choice
- Chocolate candy melts
- Colored candy melts of your choice
- Mint-flavored Life Savers
- Edible silver luster spray

Tools

- Digital scale
- Sheet pan
- Microwave-safe bowls
- Lollipop sticks
- Plastic bags
- Stiff-bristle paintbrush

1. Begin by hand weighing the cake into one-ounce portions. Shape them into teardrops and flatten the bottoms. Place them on a sheet pan in the refrigerator while you prepare the candy melts and Life Saver mints.

2. Spray the mints with the edible luster spray until silver in color and set aside to dry.

3. Melt the candy melts according to the directions on the package.

4. Remove the cake from the fridge. Dip each stick into the candy melts and insert them halfway into each cake pop. Once the candy melts have fully set and the cake is back at room temperature, you are ready to dip the pops. Fully submerge the pops into the candy melts and tap off any excess. While wet, slide a mint through the stick onto the bottom of the cake pop and attach. Allow to set.

5. Once set, using a stiff-bristle paintbrush paint on melted candy melts vertically to create the texture of the bristles.

6. Melt the candy melts of your choice in a plastic bag, snip the corner off, and pipe a small amount on the tips. Wiggle the pop gently side to side so it glides down the sides.

Paisley Cake Pops • • • • • • • • • •

Supplies

- Cake filling of your choice
- Light blue candy melts
- Red candy melts
- Black candy melts
- White candy melts

Tools

- Digital scale
- Sheet pan
- Microwave-safe bowls
- Lollipop sticks
- Plastic bags

1. Begin by hand weighing the cake into one-ounce portions. Roll them into balls and set aside on a sheet pan. Place in the fridge while you prepare the candy melts.

2. Melt the light blue and red candy melts separately, according to the directions on the package.

3. Remove the cake from the fridge. Dip each stick into the candy melts and insert them halfway into each cake pop.

4. Once the candy melts have fully set and the cake is back at room temperature, you are ready to dip the pops. Fully submerge the pops into the candy melts and tap off any excess. Place in a stand and allow to set.

5. Melt the white and black candy melts in small plastic bags and snip off the corners. Using both the black and white candy melts, pipe a paisley pattern on the pops.

Party Hat Cake Pops

Supplies

- Cake filling of your choice
- Blue candy melts
- Red candy melts
- Jumbo star sprinkles
- Red confetti sprinkles
- Red fondant

Tools

- Digital scale
- Sheet pan
- Microwave-safe bowls
- Lollipop sticks
- Plastic bag
- Pasta machine
- Numerical fondant cutters (¾-inch thick)
- Toothpicks

1. Begin by hand weighing the cake into one-ounce portions and shape them into flat triangles. Place them on a sheet pan in the refrigerator while you prepare the candy melts.

2. Melt the blue candy melts according to the directions on the package.

3. Remove the cake from the fridge. Dip each stick into the candy melts and insert them halfway into each cake pop.

4. Once the candy melts have fully set and the cake is back at room temperature, you are ready to dip the pops. Fully submerge the pops into the candy melts and tap off any excess. While still wet, place a star sprinkle on top and place in a stand. Allow to set.

5. Roll out the fondant using a pasta machine on the thickest setting and cut out any number you wish. With the use of a toothpick and candy melts, attach the number to the center of the pop and the confetti sprinkles around the pop. Allow to set.

6. Melt the red candy melts in a small plastic bag and snip off a corner. Pipe a squiggly line around the base of the pop.

Silhouette Cake Pops ● ● ● ● ● ●

Supplies

- Cake filling of your choice
- White candy melts
- Black candy melts
- Silver edible glitter
- Lemon juice or extract

Tools

- Digital scale
- Sheet pan
- Microwave-safe bowls
- Lollipop sticks
- Plastic bag
- Round cookie cutter, 1⅜ × ¾ inches
- Silhouette stencil, 1 inch in size
- Soft-bristle paintbrush

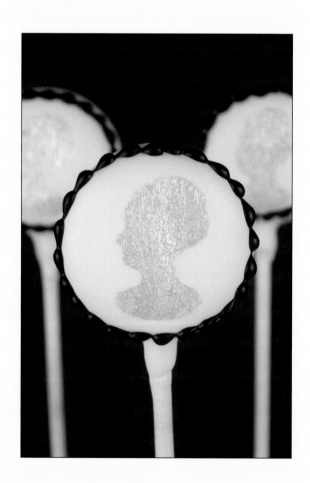

1. Stuff the cookie cutters with the cake mixture, using the palm of your hand to squeeze out any excess cake. Gently push the cakes out of the cookie cutters. Chilling your dough ahead of time makes this process easier. Place them on a sheet pan in the refrigerator while you prepare the candy melts.

2. Melt the white candy melts according to the directions on the package.

3. Remove the cake from the fridge. Dip each stick into the candy melts and insert them halfway into each cake pop.

4. Once the candy melts have fully set and the cake is back at room temperature, you are ready to dip the pops. Fully submerge the pops into the candy melts and tap off any excess. Place in a stand and allow to set.

5. Dip the tip of the soft-bristle paintbrush into the lemon juice, then into the edible glitter. Place the stencil flat on top of the pop and dab the paintbrush up and down. Keep dabbing it until you can no longer see the white candy melts. Allow to dry before removing the stencil so as to not smear the image

6. Melt the black candy melts in a small plastic bag, snip off the corner, and pipe a beaded border around the pop.

Note

Edible silver glitter has a finer texture than disco dust.

Sponge-Painted Cake Pops • • • • • • • • • • • • • • •

Supplies

- Cake filling of your choice
- Candy melts of your choice
- Pearl or petal dust of your choice
- Flavorless vodka or extract

Tools

- Digital scale
- Sheet pan
- Microwave-safe bowls
- Lollipop sticks
- Natural sponge

182

1. Begin by hand weighing the cake into one-ounce portions. Roll them into balls and flatten the tops to make flat circles. Place them on a sheet pan in the refrigerator while you prepare the candy melts.

2. Melt the candy melts according to the directions on the package.

3. Remove the cake from the fridge. Dip each stick into the candy melts and insert them halfway into each cake pop.

4. Once the candy melts have fully set and the cake is back at room temperature, you are ready to dip the pops. Fully submerge the pops into the candy melts and tap off any excess. Place in a stand and allow to set.

5. Mix the petal or pearl dust with the extract or flavorless vodka until a paintable consistency is achieved. Wet your natural sponge with water and squeeze out the excess water. Dab the sponge into your petal dust mixture and lightly dab it all over the pop and allow to dry.

Garden

Blue Bird Cake Pops ● ● ● ● ● ● ● ● ● ● ● ● ● ● ● ● ●

Supplies

- Cake filling of your choice
- White candy melts
- Blue candy melts
- Black candy melts
- Candy-coated sunflower seeds
- Orange rainbow chips

Tools

- Digital scale
- Sheet pan
- Microwave-safe bowls
- Lollipop sticks
- Plastic bags

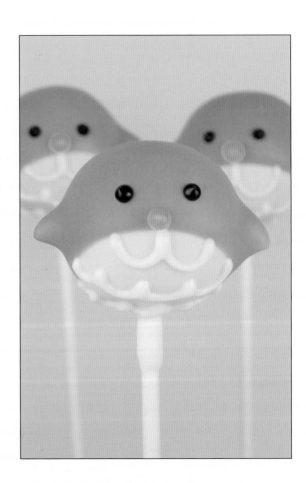

1. Begin by hand weighing the cake into one-ounce portions. Roll them into balls and set aside on a sheet pan. Place in the fridge while you prepare the candy melts.

2. Melt the white and blue candy melts according to the directions on the package.

3. Remove the cake from the fridge. Dip each stick into the candy melts and insert them halfway into each cake pop. Dip the round ends of the candy-coated sunflower seeds into the candy melts and attach to the sides of the cake for wings.

4. Once the candy melts have fully set and the cake is back at room temperature, the pops are ready to be dipped. Fully submerge the pops into the white candy melts and tap off any excess. Allow to set.

5. Dip the pops once again, but this time in the blue candy melts. Hold the pop at a 45-degree angle to make the wings. While still wet, attach an orange, rainbow chip sprinkle for the beak.

6. Melt the black and white candy melts in small plastic bags and snip off the corners. Pipe on eyes using the black candy melts. With the white melts, pipe a series of swags across the belly of the pop.

Fountain Cake Pops • • • • • • • • • • • • • • • • •

Supplies

- Cake filling of your choice
- White candy melts
- Light blue candy melts
- Green candy melts
- Brown petal dust
- Green petal dust
- Life Saver mints

Tools

- Digital scale
- Sheet pan
- Microwave-safe bowls
- Lollipop sticks
- Soft-bristle paintbrush
- Rounded tablespoon measure
- Plastic bags
- Straws

1. Use a rounded tablespoon measure as a mold for the bowl of the fountain. Stuff the cake into the measuring spoon and gently remove. To create the base of the fountain, hand weigh cake into .40-ounce portions. Roll the cake into the shape of a teardrop with a flat top instead of a pointed tip. Using a lollipop stick, create vertical indentations in the teardrop-shaped cake. Place them on a sheet pan in the refrigerator while you prepare the candy melts.

2. Melt the white candy melts according to the directions on the package.

3. Place a straw on top of a white candy melt disk and twist to create a hole in the center. This will be the base of the fountain.

4. Remove the cake from the fridge. Dip the sticks into the white candy melts and insert them completely through the teardrop-shaped cake, leaving half an inch exposed on the top. Attach a Life Saver mint on top using candy melts, allow to set, then dip the remaining exposed stick into melts and attach the cake that was molded into a bowl shape. At the base of the pop, slide the candy melt disk with the hole in the center through the stick and attach to the bottom.

5. Once the candy melts have fully set and your cake is back at room temperature, you are ready to dip the pops. Fully submerge the pop into the white candy melts and tap off any excess. Allow to set.

6. Once the pops have dried, dry dust them with the brown and green petal dust to highlight certain areas.

7. Melt the blue and green candy melts in separate plastic bags and snip off the corners. Using the blue candy melts, pipe a pool on top and dab it up and down to create texture. Pipe vines on the fountain with the green melts. A thicker consistency chocolate works best for this.

Frog Cake Pops • • • • • • • • • • • • •

Supplies

- Cake filling of your choice
- Green candy melts
- Dark green candy melts
- Black candy melts
- White Sixlets

Tools

- Digital scale
- Sheet pan
- Microwave-safe bowls
- Lollipop sticks
- Plastic bags

1. Hand weigh the cake into one-ounce portions. Roll them into balls and set aside on a sheet pan. Place in the fridge while you prepare the candy melts.

2. Melt the green candy melts according to the directions on the package.

3. Remove the cake from the fridge. Dip each stick into the candy melts and insert them halfway into each cake pop.

4. Once the candy melts have fully set and the cake is back at room temperature, the pops are ready to be dipped. Fully submerge the pops into the green candy melts and tap off any excess.

5. While the top is still wet, place two Sixlets for the eyes. Allow to fully set.

6. Melt the black and dark green candy melts in separate plastic bags, snip the corners off, and pipe on the mouth and eyes with the black candy melts. Using the dark green candy melts, pipe three dots on each cheek.

Gnome Cake Pops • • • • • • • • • • •

Supplies

- Cake filling of your choice
- Peanut butter candy melts
- White candy melts
- Black candy melts
- Red candy melts
- Sugar pearls

Tools

- Digital scale
- Sheet pan
- Microwave-safe bowls
- Lollipop sticks
- Plastic bags

1. Begin by hand weighing the cake into one-ounce portions. Shape them into tear drops. Place them on a sheet pan in the refrigerator while you prepare the candy melts.

2. Melt the peanut butter and red candy melts according to the directions on the package.

3. Remove the cake from the fridge. Dip each stick into the candy melts and insert them halfway into each cake pop. Glue a sugar pearl to the front of the pop with candy melts to create a nose.

4. Once the candy melts have fully set and the cake is back at room temperature, you are ready to dip the pops. Fully submerge the pops into the peanut butter candy melts and tap off any excess. Place in a stand and allow to set.

5. Next, dip the top half of the pop into the red candy melts and allow to set.

6. Melt the white and black candy melts in small plastic bags and snip off a corner. Using the black candy melts, pipe on two dots for the eyes near the nose. With the white candy melts, pipe on the eyebrows and beard. It is best to use slightly thick candy melts for the beard to build up the layers.

Medieval

Castle Cake Pops ⋯⋯⋯⋯

Supplies

- Cake filling of your choice
- Gray candy melts
- Black candy melts
- Green candy melts
- Fondant
- Black petal dust

Tools

- Digital scale
- Sheet pan
- Microwave-safe bowls
- Lollipop sticks
- Plastic bags
- Soft-bristle paintbrush
- Pasta machine
- #1 ¾-inch fondant cutter

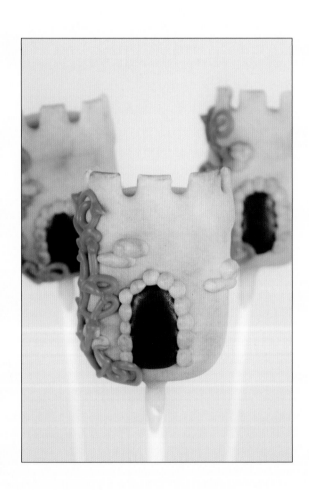

1. Begin by hand weighing the cake into one-ounce portions. Shape them into rectangular logs approximately 1½ × 1 inches. Place them on a sheet pan in the refrigerator while you prepare the candy melts and fondant.

2. Roll out the fondant on the thickest setting, then cut it into half-inch-wide strips long enough to wrap around the top of your cake. Using the #1 fondant cutter, cut out small notches from the top of the fondant.

3. Melt the candy melts according to the directions on the package.

4. Remove the cake from the fridge. Dip each stick into the candy melts and insert them halfway into each cake pop. Place some candy melts on the fondant strips and attach to the cake.

5. Once the candy melts have fully set and the cake is back at room temperature, you are ready to dip the pops. Fully submerge the pops into the candy melts and tap off any excess. Allow to set.

6. Prepare gray, black, and green candy melts in plastic bags, snip off the corners, and, using the gray melts, pipe bricks as well as dots around where the door will go. Allow to set.

7. Once set using a soft-bristle paintbrush lightly dust the pops with black petal dust.

8. Using the black melts, flood the doorway and allow to set. With the green melts pipe vines and leaves along one side of the pop.

Dragon Cake Pops ● ● ● ● ● ● ● ●

Supplies

- Cake filling of your choice
- Red candy melts
- Black candy melts
- White candy melts
- Red jumbo star sprinkles

Tools

- Digital scale
- Sheet pan
- Microwave-safe bowls
- Lollipop sticks
- Plastic bags

1. Hand weigh the cake into one-ounce portions and shape into pears. Place them on a sheet pan in the refrigerator while you prepare the candy melts.

2. Melt the red candy melts according to the directions on the package.

3. Remove the cake from the fridge. Dip each stick into the candy melts and insert them halfway into each cake pop.

4. Once the candy melts have fully set and the cake is back at room temperature, you are ready to dip the pops. Fully submerge the pops into the candy melts and tap off any excess.

5. While still wet, insert three star sprinkles into the back of the head. Allow to set.

6. Melt the black and white candy melts in separate small plastic bags and snip off the corners. Pipe on eyes, nostrils, and a smile. Using the white candy melts, pipe on teeth; this works best with thicker candy melts.

Knight Cake Pops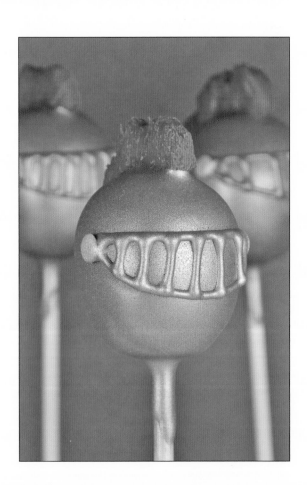

Supplies

- Cake filling of your choice
- Gray candy melts
- Red candy melts
- White confetti sprinkles
- Smarties
- Edible silver luster spray

Tools

- Digital scale
- Sheet pan
- Microwave-safe bowls
- Lollipop sticks
- Plastic bag
- Stiff-bristle paintbrush

1. Begin by hand weighing the cake into one-ounce portions. Roll them into balls and slightly elongate them and taper the bottom. Place them on a sheet pan in the refrigerator while you prepare the candy melts.

2. Melt the gray candy melts according to the directions on the package.

3. Remove the cake from the fridge. Dip each stick into the candy melts and insert them halfway into each cake pop. Dip three Smarties into the candy melts and attach to the top of the cake.

4. Once the candy melts have fully set and the cake is back at room temperature, the pops are ready to be dipped. Fully submerge the pops into the gray candy melts and tap off any excess. Allow to set.

5. Prepare the gray candy melts in a plastic bag, snip off a corner, and pipe the face guard onto the pop. While still wet, attach a white confetti sprinkle on each side of the pop.

6. Once the candy melts have hardened, spray the pops with the edible luster spray until silver in color.

7. When the spray has dried, paint the red candy melts on top of the Smarties using the stiff-bristle paintbrush to add texture.

Music

Drum Cake Pops • • • • • • • • • • •

Supplies

- Cake filling of your choice
- Red candy melts
- White candy melts
- Fondant
- Silver luster dust

Tools

- Digital scale
- Sheet pan
- Microwave-safe bowls
- Lollipop sticks
- Plastic bags
- Pasta machine
- Soft-bristle paintbrush

1. Begin by hand weighing the cake into one-ounce portions. Shape them into drums. Place them on a sheet pan in the refrigerator while you prepare the candy melts.

2. Melt the red and white candy melts according to the directions on the package.

3. Remove the cake from the fridge. Dip each stick into the candy melts and insert them halfway into each cake pop.

4. Once the candy melts have fully set and the cake is back at room temperature, you are ready to dip the pops. Fully submerge the pops into the red candy melts and tap off any excess. Allow to set.

5. Once set, dip just the tops of the pops into the white candy melts. Allow to set.

6. Roll out the fondant on the thickest setting and cut it into ¼-inch-wide strips that are long enough to wrap around the pop. Each pop will require two strips.

7. Using the soft-bristle paintbrush, dust the fondant strips with the silver luster dust.

8. Attach candy melts to the back of the strips and attach them to the top and bottom of each pop.

9. Melt the white candy melts in a plastic bag, snip off the corner, and pipe a zigzag in the middle of the pop.

Microphone Cake Pops • • • • • • • • • • • • • • • • • •

Supplies

- Cake filling of your choice
- Black candy melts
- Silver sprinkles

Tools

- Digital scale
- Sheet pan
- Microwave-safe bowls
- Lollipop sticks
- Plastic bag

1. Begin by hand weighing the cake into one-ounce portions, then separate those into .40-ounce and .60-ounce portions. Roll the .60-ounce pieces into balls and set aside on a sheet pan. Roll the .40-ounce pieces into cylinders approximately 1½ inches long to make the handles of the microphones. Place in the fridge while you prepare the candy melts.

2. Melt the black candy melts according to the directions on the package.

3. Remove the cake from the fridge. Dip the sticks into the candy melts and insert them completely through the cylinder portions of the cake, exposing half an inch of the stick. Dip the exposed sticks into candy melts once again and place the .60-ounce balls on top.

4. Once the candy melts have fully set and the cake is back at room temperature, you are ready to dip the pops. Fully submerge the pops into the black candy melts and tap off any excess. Place in a stand and allow to set.

5. After the pops have set, once again dip the pops into the candy melts, this time only the top ball portion. Tap off the excess and sprinkle the silver sprinkles over the wet candy melts and allow to set.

6. Once set, pipe two dots onto the handle for buttons, using the black candy melts.

Music Note Cake Pops

Supplies

- Cake filling of your choice
- White candy melts
- Black candy melts

Tools

- Digital scale
- Sheet pan
- Microwave-safe bowls
- Lollipop sticks
- Plastic bag

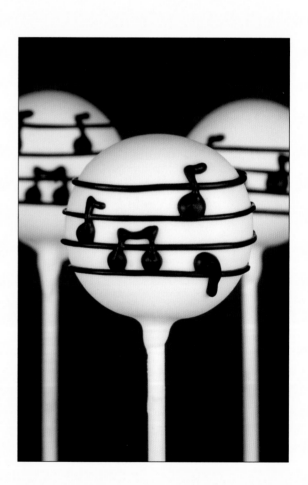

1. Begin by hand weighing the cake into one-ounce portions. Roll them into balls and flatten the tops until you have flat circles. Place them on a sheet pan in the refrigerator while you prepare the candy melts.

2. Melt the white candy melts according to the directions on the package.

3. Remove the cake from the fridge. Dip each stick into the candy melts and insert them halfway into each cake pop.

4. Once the candy melts have fully set and the cake is back at room temperature, you are ready to dip the pops. Fully submerge the pops into the candy melts and tap off any excess. Place in a stand and allow to set.

5. Melt the black candy melts in a small plastic bag and snip off a corner. Pipe four horizontal lines and allow to set. Once set, pipe on various music notes.

Nature

Cloud Cake Pops • • • • • • • • • •

Supplies

- Cake filling of your choice
- White candy melts

Tools

- Digital scale
- Sheet pan
- Microwave-safe bowls
- Lollipop sticks
- Plastic bag
- 1½ × 1¾ inch cloud-shaped cookie cutter

1. Stuff the cookie cutter with the cake mixture, using the palm of your hand to squeeze out any excess cake. Gently push the cake out of the cookie cutter. Chilling your dough ahead of time makes this process easier. Place them on a sheet pan in the refrigerator while you prepare the candy melts.

2. Melt the white candy melts according to the directions on the package.

3. Remove the cake from the fridge. Dip each stick into the candy melts and insert them halfway into each cake pop.

4. Once the candy melts have fully set and the cake is back at room temperature, you are ready to dip the pops. Fully submerge the pops into the candy melts and tap off any excess. Place in a stand and allow to set.

5. Melt the white candy melts in a small plastic bag and snip off a corner. Pipe and swirl the candy melts on top of the pop.

Flame Cake Pops ● ● ● ● ● ● ● ● ● ●

Supplies

- Cake filling of your choice
- White candy melts
- Orange candy melts
- Yellow candy melts
- Red candy melts

Tools

- Digital scale
- Sheet pan
- Microwave-safe bowls
- Lollipop sticks
- Plastic bags
- Toothpick

1. Begin by hand weighing the cake into one-ounce portions. Roll them into balls and flatten the tops until you have rounded flat circles. Place them on a sheet pan in the refrigerator for a few minutes while you prepare the candy melts.

2. Melt the white candy melts according to the directions on the package.

3. Remove the cake from the fridge. Dip each stick into the candy melts and insert it halfway into each cake pop.

4. Once the candy melts have fully set and the cake is back at room temperature, you are ready to dip the pops. Fully submerge the pops into the candy melts and tap off any excess. Place in a stand and allow to set.

5. Melt the red, yellow, and orange candy melts in one plastic bag. Swirl the colors together and snip off a corner. Pipe a puddle of candy melts on the base around the stick. Drag a toothpick through the candy melts toward the top of the pop to create the flames and allow to set.

Note

If you want the flames to stick out, dip the pops in black candy melts instead of white.

Hydrangea Cake Pops • • • • • • • • • • • • • • • • • • •

Supplies

- Cake filling of your choice
- Green candy melts
- White candy melts
- Sugar pearls
- Yellow petal dust
- Fondant

Tools

- Digital scale
- Sheet pan
- Microwave-safe bowls
- Lollipop sticks
- Plastic bag
- Toothpick
- Soft-bristle paintbrush
- Pasta machine
- Hydrangea plunger and
  impression mat, 1-inch in size

1. Ahead of time, roll out fondant using the thickest setting on a pasta machine. Using the flower plunger, cut out flowers and press firmly into the impression mat to create the shape of the flower. Set aside and let dry.

2. Once the fondant flowers are dry, dust the centers with the yellow petal dust using the soft-bristle paintbrush. Melt some white candy melts and add a dot to the center of the flower with a toothpick. Attach a sugar pearl and allow to set.

3. Hand weigh the cake into one-ounce portions. Roll them into balls and set aside on a sheet pan. Place them in the fridge for a few minutes while you prepare the green candy melts.

4. Remove the cake from the fridge. Dip each stick into the candy melts and insert them halfway into each cake pop.

5. Once the candy melts have fully set and the cake is back at room temperature, you are ready to dip the pops. Fully submerge the pops into the green candy melts and tap off any excess. Allow to set.

6. Create texture by dabbing the candy melts all over using a soft-bristle paintbrush. Allow to set.

7. Prepare the green candy melts in a small plastic bag, snip off the corner, and pipe vines around the pops. Attach the fondant flowers to the top and allow to set. Lastly, pipe on leaves.

Rainbow Cake Pops ● ● ● ● ● ● ●

Supplies

- Red cake filling
- Yellow cake filling
- Green cake filling
- Blue cake filling
- Light blue candy melts
- Red candy melts
- Orange candy melts
- Yellow candy melts
- Green candy melts
- Blue candy melts
- White candy melts

Tools

- Digital scale
- Sheet pan
- Microwave-safe bowls
- Lollipop sticks
- Plastic bags

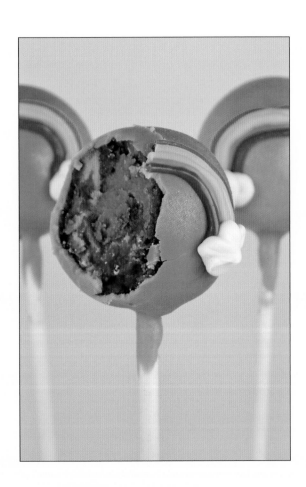

1. Roll the different color cakes together into one-ounce balls to create swirls. Place them on a sheet pan in the refrigerator while you prepare the candy melts.

2. Melt the light blue candy melts according to the directions on the package.

3. Remove the cake balls from the fridge. Dip each stick into the candy melts and insert them halfway into each cake pop.

4. Once the candy melts have fully set and the cake is back at room temperature, you are ready to dip the pops. Fully submerge the pops into the candy melts and tap off any excess. Allow to set.

5. Melt the red, orange, yellow, green, blue, and white candy melts in separate plastic bags, snip off the corners, and pipe on the colors of the rainbow. Then pipe on clouds using the white candy melts, which should have a thicker consistency.

Rose Cake Pops • • • • • • • • • • •

Supplies

- Cake filling of your choice
- White candy melts
- Yellow sanding sugar
- 1-inch fondant roses

Tools

- Digital scale
- Sheet pan
- Microwave-safe bowls
- Lollipop sticks
- Plastic bag

1. Begin by hand weighing the cake into one-ounce portions. Roll them into balls and set aside on a sheet pan. Place in the fridge while you prepare the candy melts.

2. Melt the white candy melts according to the directions on the package.

3. Remove the cake from the fridge. Dip each stick into the candy melts and insert them halfway into each cake pop.

4. Once the candy melts have fully set and the cake is back at room temperature, the pops are ready to be dipped. Fully submerge the pops into the white candy melts and tap off any excess. While still wet, sprinkle the sanding sugar on top and attach a fondant rose. Allow to set.

Pirates

Doubloon Cake Pops • • • • • • •

Supplies

- Cake filling of your choice
- Yellow candy melts
- Bone sprinkles
- Skull sprinkles
- Fondant
- Edible gold luster spray

Tools

- Digital scale
- Sheet pan
- Microwave-safe bowls
- Lollipop sticks
- Pasta machine
- Numerical fondant cutters – ¾-inch thick
- Toothpicks

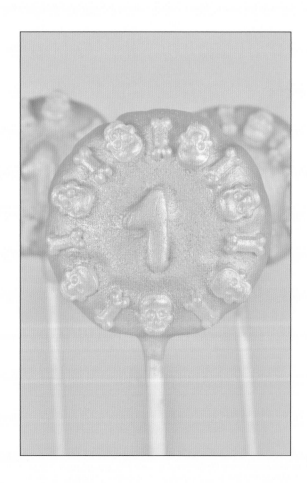

1. Begin by hand weighing the cake into one-ounce portions. Roll them into balls and flatten the tops until you have flat circles. Place them on a sheet pan in the refrigerator while you prepare the candy melts.

2. Melt the yellow candy melts according to the directions on the package. Remove the cake from the fridge. Dip each stick into the candy melts and insert them halfway into each cake pop.

3. Once the candy melts have fully set and the cake is back at room temperature, you are ready to dip the pops. Fully submerge the pops into the candy melts and tap off any excess. Place in a stand and allow to set.

4. Roll out the fondant using a pasta machine on the thickest setting and cut out any number you wish. With a toothpick and candy melts, attach the number to the center of the pop as well as the bones and skulls around the edge. Allow to set.

5. Using the edible gold luster spray, spray the entire pop until gold in color.

Pirate Cake Pops ● ● ● ● ● ● ● ● ●

Supplies

- Cake filling of your choice
- Peanut butter candy melts
- Black candy melts
- Red candy melts
- White confetti sprinkles
- Gold luster dust

Tools

- Digital scale
- Sheet pan
- Microwave-safe bowls
- Lollipop sticks
- Plastic bags
- Soft-bristle paintbrush

1. Begin by hand weighing the cake into one-ounce portions. Roll them into balls and set aside on a sheet pan. Place in the fridge while you prepare the candy melts.

2. Melt the peanut butter and red candy melts according to the directions on the package.

3. Remove the cake from the fridge. Dip each stick into the candy melts and insert them halfway into each cake pop. Slightly dip the tips of two confetti sprinkles into candy melts and insert them to the sides of the cake to create ears.

4. Once the candy melts have fully set and the cake is back at room temperature, you are ready to dip the pops. Fully submerge the pops into the peanut butter candy melts and tap off any excess. Place in a stand and allow to set.

5. Next, dip the top half of the pop into the red candy melts. While still wet, attach white confetti sprinkles to the top.

6. Melt peanut butter, white, and black candy melts in separate small plastic bags and snip off the corners. Pipe on the nose with peanut butter candy melts, the facial hair and eye patch with black candy melts, and attach a white confetti sprinkle for the eye, piping a black dot in the center.

7. Dust on a few white confetti sprinkles with gold luster dust to create earrings and attach to an ear with the use of candy melts.

Skull Cake Pops　• • • • • • • • • • •

Supplies

- Cake filling of your choice
- White candy melts
- Black candy melts

Tools

- Digital scale
- Sheet pan
- Microwave-safe bowls
- Lollipop sticks
- Plastic bag
- 1½-inch skull-shaped cookie cutter

1. Stuff the cookie cutter with the cake mixture, using the palm of your hand to squeeze out any excess cake. Gently push the cake out of the cookie cutter. Chilling your dough ahead of time makes this process easier. Place them on a sheet pan in the refrigerator while you prepare the candy melts.

2. Melt the white candy melts according to the directions on the package.

3. Remove the cake from the fridge. Dip each stick into the candy melts and insert them halfway into each cake pop.

4. Once the candy melts have fully set and the cake is back at room temperature, you are ready to dip the pops. Fully submerge the pops into the candy melts and tap off any excess. Place in a stand and allow to set.

5. Melt the black candy melts in a small plastic bag and snip off a corner. Pipe the eyes, nose, and mouth onto the pop and allow to set.

Treasure Chest
Cake Pops • • • • • • • • • • • • • •

Supplies

- Cake filling of your choice
- Yellow candy melts
- Gold sprinkles
- Small confetti sprinkles
- Sugar pearls
- White fondant
- Black fondant
- Brown food coloring
- Lemon juice or extract
- Gold luster spray
- Black confetti sprinkles

Tools

- Digital scale
- Sheet pan
- Microwave-safe bowls
- Lollipop sticks
- Plastic bags
- Pasta machine
- Soft-bristle paintbrush
- Wood-grain fondant impression mat

1. Begin by hand weighing the cake into one-ounce portions. Shape them into rectangles approximately 1½ × 1 inch wide. Place them on a sheet pan in the refrigerator while you prepare the candy melts.

2. Melt the yellow candy melts according to the directions on the package.

3. Remove the cake from the fridge. Dip each stick into the candy melts and insert them halfway into each cake pop.

4. Once the candy melts have fully set and the cake is back at room temperature, you are ready to dip the pops. Fully submerge the pops into the yellow candy melts and tap off any excess. While wet, sprinkle gold and confetti sprinkles on top. Allow to set.

5. Once set, spray the top with the gold luster spray and allow to dry.

6. Roll out the fondant on the thickest setting and imprint the fondant using the wood-grain mat. Cut the fondant wide and long enough to wrap around the pop, leaving a small opening around the top.

7. Add a small amount of lemon juice or extract to the brown food coloring and mix. Using a soft-bristle paintbrush, paint the fondant strips with the food coloring and allow to dry.

8. Roll out the black fondant on the thinnest setting and cut into ⅛-inch-wide strips that are as long as the treasure chest is tall. Attach with candy melts and attach a black confetti sprinkle in the center.

9. Using candy melts, attach and wrap the wood grain strips to the pop. Sprinkle sugar pearls on top.

Safari

Elephant Cake Pops • • • • • • • •

Supplies

- Cake filling of your choice
- Gray candy melts
- Black candy melts
- Candy melt disk
- Fondant

Tools

- Digital scale
- Sheet pan
- Microwave-safe bowls
- Lollipop sticks

1. Ahead of time, roll out two small cones per pop from the fondant for the tusks and allow to harden.

2. Hand weigh the cake into one-ounce portions. Roll them into balls and elongate them to create the trunk. Place in the fridge while you prepare the candy melts.

3. Melt the candy melts according to the directions on the package.

4. Remove the cake from the fridge. Dip each stick into the candy melts and insert them halfway into each cake pop, through the tip of the trunk. Attach a candy melt disk on each side of the cake for the ears.

5. Once the candy melts have fully set and the cake is back at room temperature, you are ready to dip the pops. Fully submerge the pops into the candy melts and tap off any excess. While wet, attach the tusks to the sides of the trunk and allow to set.

6. Prepare the black candy melts in a small plastic bag, snip off a corner, and pipe two dots for the eyes.

Giraffe Cake Pops ●●●●●●●●

Supplies

- Cake filling of your choice
- Yellow candy melts
- Brown candy melts
- Black candy melts
- Sprinkle sparks
- Fondant

Tools

- Digital scale
- Sheet pan
- Microwave-safe bowls
- Lollipop sticks
- Plastic bag
- ¾-inch rose petal cutter
- Pasta machine

1. Roll out the fondant ahead of time on the thickest setting and cut out two petals per pop with the small rose petal cutter. Pinch the rounded ends together and allow to fully harden.

2. Hand weigh the cake into one-ounce portions. Roll them into balls and sculpt into pear shapes. Place them on a sheet pan in the refrigerator while you prepare the candy melts.

3. Melt the yellow candy melts according to the directions on the package.

4. Remove the cake from the fridge. Dip the sticks into the candy melts and insert them halfway into the cake, at a slight angle, in the back of the narrow portion. Dip the pinched section of ears created earlier as well as the sprinkle sparks into the candy melts and attach to the tops of the heads.

5. Once the candy melts have fully set and the cake is back at room temperature, the pops are ready to be dipped. Fully submerge the pops into the yellow candy melts and tap off any excess. Allow to set in a stand.

6. While the pops are drying, melt the chocolate candy melts according to the directions on the package. Once dried, slightly dip the bottom portion of the pop to create the snout and allow to set.

7. Melt the chocolate and black candy melts in separate plastic bags and snip off the corners. Use the chocolate melts to pipe on spots, eyebrows, the inner ears, hair, and a dot on each horn. Pipe the eyes and mouth with the black melts. Allow to set.

Hippo Cake Pops •••••••••••

Supplies

- Cake filling of your choice
- Purple candy melts
- Black candy melts
- White candy melts
- Red Hots candy

Tools

- Digital scale
- Sheet pan
- Microwave-safe bowls
- Lollipop sticks
- Plastic bag

1. Hand weigh the cake into one-ounce portions. Roll them into balls and sculpt into pear shapes. Place them on a sheet pan in the refrigerator while you prepare the candy melts.

2. Melt the purple candy melts according to the directions on the package.

3. Remove the cake from the fridge. Dip the sticks into the candy melts and insert them halfway into the cake, at a slight angle, in the back of the narrow portion. Dip the Red Hots into the candy melts and attach to the tops of the heads for ears.

4. Once the candy melts have fully set and the cake is back at room temperature, the pops are ready to be dipped. Fully submerge the pops into the purple candy melts and tap off any excess. Allow to set in a stand.

5. Melt the black and white candy melts in separate plastic bags and snip off the corners. Using the black melts, pipe on two small dots for the eyes, two larger dots for the nostrils, and a smile. Allow to set. Pipe on two teeth with the white melts.

Note

When dipping pops in which the stick is inserted at an angle, instead of directly into the bottom, always tap off excess candy melts with the wider, top half facing you.

Lion Cake Pops •••••••••••••••

Supplies

- Cake filling of your choice
- Peanut butter candy melts
- Chocolate candy melts
- White candy melts
- Black candy melts
- Pink candy melts
- Smarties

Tools

- Digital scale
- Sheet pan
- Microwave-safe bowls
- Lollipop sticks
- Plastic bags

1. Begin by hand weighing the cake into one-ounce portions. Roll them into balls and set aside on a sheet pan. Place in the fridge while you prepare the candy melts.

2. Melt the peanut butter candy melts according to the directions on the package.

3. Remove the cake from the fridge. Dip each stick into the candy melts and insert them halfway into each cake pop. Dip two Smarties into the melts and attach at the top of each of the cake pops for the ears.

4. Once the candy melts have fully set and the cake is back at room temperature, you are ready to dip the pops. Fully submerge the pops into the candy melts and tap off any excess. Place in a stand and allow to set.

5. Melt the chocolate, pink, white, and black candy melts in separate small plastic bags and snip off the corners. Using the pink candy melts, pipe a dot in each ear. With the white candy melts, pipe two dots onto the face to create cheeks. Pipe them slightly apart so when the pop is tapped to smooth out the candy melts they barely touch. Allow to set.

6. Once set, pipe the nose, two dots for the eyes, and three smaller dots on each cheek with the black candy melts. Using the chocolate candy melts, pipe on strands of fur going around the pop to create the mane. Do this in layers to achieve a full mane; allow each layer to fully set before piping an additional layer.

Tiger Cake Pops • • • • • • • • • • • •

Supplies

- Cake filling of your choice
- Orange candy melts
- White candy melts
- Black candy melts
- Pink candy melts
- Mini heart sprinkles
- Smarties

Tools

- Digital scale
- Sheet pan
- Microwave-safe bowls
- Lollipop sticks
- Plastic bags

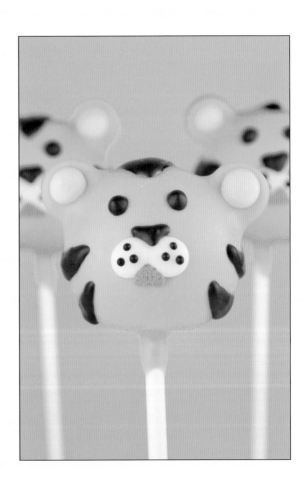

1. Begin by hand weighing the cake into one-ounce portions. Roll them into balls and set aside on a sheet pan. Place in the fridge while you prepare the candy melts.

2. Melt the orange candy melts according to the directions on the package.

3. Remove the cake from the fridge. Dip each stick into the candy melts and insert them halfway into each cake pop. Dip two Smarties into the melts and attach at the top of each of the cake pops for the ears.

4. Once the candy melts have fully set and the cake is back at room temperature, you are ready to dip the pops. Fully submerge the pops into the candy melts and tap off any excess. Place in a stand and allow to set.

5. Melt the pink, white, and black candy melts in separate small plastic bags and snip off the corners. Using the pink candy melts pipe a dot in each ear. With the white candy melts pipe two dots onto the face to create cheeks. Pipe them slightly apart so when the pop is tapped to smooth out the candy melts they barely touch. While still wet, attach a heart sprinkle in between the two dots. Allow to set.

6. Once set, pipe the nose, two dots for the eyes, and three smaller dots on each cheek with the black candy melts, as well as stripes on the top and sides of the head.

Zebra Cake Pops

Supplies

- Cake filling of your choice
- White candy melts
- Black candy melts
- Pink candy melts
- Smarties

Tools

- Digital scale
- Sheet pan
- Microwave-safe bowls
- Lollipop sticks
- Plastic bag
- Stiff-bristle paintbrush

1. Hand weigh the cake into one-ounce portions. Roll them into balls and sculpt into pear shapes. Place them on a sheet pan in the refrigerator while you prepare the candy melts.

2. Melt the white candy melts according to the directions on the package.

3. Remove the cake from the fridge. Dip the sticks into the candy melts and insert them halfway into the cake, at a slight angle, in the back of the narrow portion. Dip the five Smarties into the candy melts and attach to the tops of the heads—two for the ears and three for the mane.

4. Once the candy melts have fully set and the cake is back at room temperature, the pops are ready to be dipped. Fully submerge the pops into the white candy melts and tap off any excess. Allow to set in a stand.

5. While the pops are drying, melt the pink candy melts according to the directions on the package. Once dried, slightly dip the bottom portion of the pop to create the snout and allow to set. Using the same melts, dot on the inner ears.

6. Melt the black and white candy melts in separate plastic bags and snip off the corners. Using the black melts, pipe two stripes on each side of the face, the eyes, nostrils, and mouth. Allow to set. Using a stiff-bristle paintbrush, paint black and white candy melts onto the mane to texture it.

Space

Alien Cake Pops

Supplies

- Cake filling of your choice
- Green candy melts
- Yellow candy melts
- White candy melts
- Black candy melts

Tools

- Digital scale
- Sheet pan
- Microwave-safe bowls
- Lollipop sticks
- Plastic bags
- Soft-bristle paintbrush
- 2-inch gingerbread man–shaped cookie cutter

1. Stuff the cookie cutter with the cake mixture, using the palm of your hand to squeeze out any excess cake. Gently push the cake out of the cookie cutter. Chilling your dough ahead of time makes this process easier. Slightly flatten the cake to soften the edges. Place the cake pops on a sheet pan in the refrigerator while you prepare the candy melts.

2. Melt the green candy melts according to the directions on the package.

3. Remove the cake from the fridge. Dip each stick into the candy melts and insert them halfway into each cake pop.

4. Once the candy melts have fully set and the cake is back at room temperature, you are ready to dip the pops. Fully submerge the pops into the green candy melts and tap off any excess. Place in a stand and allow to set.

5. Dab on candy melts all over the pop using a soft-bristle paintbrush to create texture on the pops.

6. Melt the yellow, white, and black candy melts in separate small plastic bags and snip off the corners. Using the white candy melts, pipe a dot onto the head and, while still wet, pipe a black dot in the center. With the yellow candy melts, pipe a circle in the center of the body and allow to set. Once set, pipe swags over the belly and pipe nails on the hands and feet.

Astronaut Cake Pops ·······

Supplies

- Cake filling of your choice
- White candy melts
- Black candy melts
- Peanut butter candy melts
- Red fondant

Tools

- Digital scale
- Sheet pan
- Microwave-safe bowls
- Lollipop sticks
- Plastic bags
- Pasta machine
- Piping tip

1. Hand weigh the cake into .80-ounce and .20-ounce portions. Roll them into balls and flatten the .20-ounce ball. Place them on a sheet pan in the refrigerator while you prepare the candy melts.

2. Melt the white and peanut butter candy melts according to the directions on the package.

3. Remove the cake from the fridge. Dip the sticks into the candy melts and insert them completely through the .20-ounce portion and halfway into the .80-ounce portion.

4. Once the candy melts have fully set and the cake is back at room temperature, the pops are ready to be dipped. Fully submerge the pops into the white candy melts and tap off any excess. Allow to set in a stand.

5. Gently tap the upper ball into a spoonful of peanut butter candy melts to create the face. Allow the excess to fall off, invert, and gently shake side to side to smooth out the face. Set aside to dry.

6. While the pops are drying, roll out the fondant on the thick setting using a pasta machine. Using the piping tips as a cutter, cut out two circles per pop and attach them on either side of each pop.

7. Melt the white and black candy melts according to the directions on the package. Outline the face with the white candy melts and pipe a line around where the two portions of cake meet. Using the black candy melts, pipe on the hair, eyes, and mouth.

Meteor Cake Pops · · · · · · · · · ·

Supplies

- Cake filling of your choice
- Gray candy melts
- Black petal dust

Tools

- Digital scale
- Sheet pan
- Microwave-safe bowls
- Lollipop sticks
- Soft-bristle paintbrush

1. Begin by hand weighing the cake into one-ounce portions. Roll them into balls and set aside on a sheet pan. Place in the fridge while you prepare the candy melts.

2. Melt the gray candy melts according to the directions on the package.

3. Remove the cake from the fridge. Dip each stick into the candy melts and insert them halfway into each cake pop. Using the tip of a lollipop stick, create various indentations and craters on the surface.

4. Once the candy melts have fully set and the cake is back at room temperature, you are ready to dip the pops. Fully submerge the pops into the candy melts and tap off any excess. Place in a stand and allow to set.

5. With the soft-bristle paintbrush, lightly dust the entire pop, highlighting the craters with the black petal dust.

Midnight Sky Cake Pops

● ● ● ● ● ● ● ● ● ● ● ● ● ● ● ●

Supplies

- Cake filling of your choice
- Dark blue candy melts
- Disco dust
- Black petal dust
- Gold luster dust
- Mini star sprinkles

Tools

- Digital scale
- Sheet pan
- Microwave-safe bowls
- Lollipop sticks
- Plastic bags
- Toothpick
- Soft-bristle paintbrush

254

1. Begin by hand weighing the cake into one-ounce portions. Roll them into balls and flatten the tops until you have flat circles. Place them on a sheet pan in the refrigerator for a few minutes while you prepare the candy melts.

2. Melt the dark blue candy melts according to the directions on the package.

3. Remove the cake from the fridge. Dip each stick into the candy melts and insert them halfway into each cake pop.

4. Once the candy melts have fully set and the cake is back at room temperature, you are ready to dip the pops. Fully submerge the pops into the candy melts and tap off any excess.

5. While still wet, sprinkle the front of the pops with disco dust and allow to set.

6. Once the pops have set, lightly dust them with black petal dust to create color variation in the sky.

7. In a plastic bag, mix the yellow star sprinkles with the gold petal dust and shake the bag until all the stars are gold in color.

8. With a toothpick, dot on candy melts and attach the stars to the pop.

UFO Cake Pops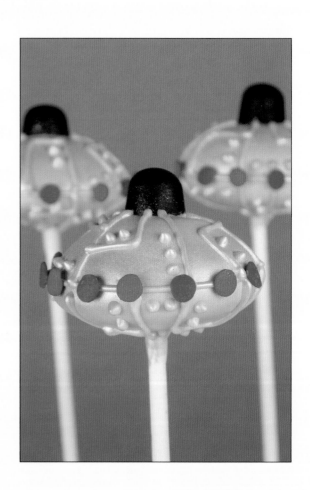

Supplies

- Cake filling of your choice
- Gray candy melts
- Silver luster dust
- Black gumdrops
- Mini red confetti sprinkles
- Mini green confetti sprinkles

Tools

- Digital scale
- Sheet pan
- Microwave-safe bowls
- Lollipop sticks
- Plastic bags
- Toothpicks
- Soft-bristle paintbrushes

1. Begin by hand weighing the cake into one-ounce portions. Roll them into a ball and flatten the tops of them until you have rounded, flat circles. Pinch the rims of the circles to slightly sharpen them. Place them on a sheet pan in the refrigerator while you prepare the candy melts.

2. Cut the black gumdrops in half horizontally, toss the bottoms out, and only keep the tops.

3. Melt the candy melts according to the directions on the package.

4. Remove the cake from the fridge. Dip each stick into the candy melts and insert them halfway into each cake pop.

5. Once the candy melts have fully set and the cake is back at room temperature, you are ready to dip the pops. Fully submerge the pops into the candy melts and tap off any excess. While wet, attach the gumdrops to the tops of the pops. Place in a stand and allow to set.

6. Prepare some of the gray candy melts in a plastic bag, snip off the corner, and pipe a series of lines and dots onto the tops to create panels and rivets. Allow to set.

7. Once set dry dust the pop with silver luster dust.

8. Attach the green and red sprinkles using toothpicks and candy melts around the middle of the cake pop.

Sports and Games

Arrow Head Cake Pops • • • • • • • • • • • • • • • • •

Supplies

- Cake filling of your choice
- Chocolate candy melts
- Silver luster dust
- Black petal dust

Tools

- Digital scale
- Sheet pan
- Microwave-safe bowls
- Lollipop sticks
- Soft-bristle paintbrush
- Aluminum foil
- 1½-inch tree-shaped cookie cutter

1. Stuff the cookie cutter with the cake mixture, using the palm of your hand to squeeze out any excess cake. Gently push the cake out of the cookie cutter. Chilling your dough ahead of time makes this process easier. Flatten the cake as much as possible while still maintaining the basic shape.

2. Crumple up a piece of aluminum foil into a ball and roll it all over the cake to texture it. Set the cake balls aside on a sheet pan and place in the fridge while you prepare the candy melts.

3. Melt the chocolate candy melts according to the directions on the package.

4. Remove the cake from the fridge. Dip each stick into the candy melts and insert them halfway into each cake pop.

5. Once the candy melts have fully set and the cake is back at room temperature, you are ready to dip the pops. Fully submerge the pops into the candy melts and tap off any excess. Place in a stand and allow to set.

6. Using a soft-bristle paintbrush, lightly dust the pops with the silver luster dust and black petal dust.

Ballet Slipper Cake Pops • • • • • • • • • • • • • • • •

Supplies

- Cake filling of your choice
- White candy melts
- Pink candy melts

Tools

- Digital scale
- Sheet pan
- Microwave-safe bowls
- Lollipop sticks
- Plastic bag

1. Begin by hand weighing the cake into one-ounce portions. Roll them into balls and slightly elongate them to resemble a slipper. Place them on a sheet pan in the refrigerator while you prepare the candy melts.

2. Melt the white and pink candy melts according to the directions on the package.

3. Remove the cake from the fridge. Dip each stick into the candy melts and insert them halfway into each cake pop.

4. Once the candy melts have fully set and the cake is back at room temperature, the pops are ready to be dipped. Fully submerge the pops into the white candy melts and tap off any excess. Allow to set.

5. Once the white candy melts have set, dip the pops once again, but this time in the pink candy melts. Dip the pop at a 45-degree angle until the candy melts cover the front and sides of the pop while still exposing some of the white candy melts. Place in a stand and allow to set.

6. Prepare the pink candy melts in a plastic bag, snip off a corner, and pipe on laces.

Dice Cake Pops • • • • • • • • • • •

Supplies

- Cake filling of your choice
- White candy melts
- Black candy melts

Tools

- Digital scale
- Sheet pan
- Microwave-safe bowls
- Lollipop sticks
- Plastic bag

1. Begin by hand weighing the cake into one-ounce portions. Roll them into balls and shape into a cube using a flat surface, rotating and flattening each rounded edge. Place them on a sheet pan in the refrigerator for a few minutes while you prepare the candy melts.

2. Melt the white candy melts according to the directions on the package.

3. Remove the cake from the fridge. Dip each stick into the candy melts and insert them halfway into each cake pop.

4. Once the candy melts have fully set and the cake is back at room temperature, you are ready to dip the pops. Fully submerge the pops into the candy melts and tap off any excess. Place in a stand and allow to set.

5. In a plastic bag, melt the black candy melts and snip off the corner. Pipe dots on each side of the pop for the dice numbers

Note

If you don't want to pipe the black dots, you can also use small black confetti sprinkles.

Domino Cake Pops • • • • • • • •

Supplies

- Cake filling of your choice
- White candy melts
- Black candy melts

Tools

- Digital scale
- Sheet pan
- Microwave-safe bowls
- Lollipop sticks
- Plastic bag

1. Begin by hand weighing the cake into one-ounce portions. Shape them into rectangles approximately 1½ × 1 inch in size and set them aside on a sheet pan. Place in the fridge while you prepare the candy melts.

2. Melt the white candy melts according to the directions on the package.

3. Remove the cake from the fridge. Dip each stick into the candy melts and insert them halfway into each cake pop.

4. Once the candy melts have fully set and the cake is back at room temperature, you are ready to dip the pops. Fully submerge the pops into the candy melts and tap off any excess. Place the pops into a stand and allow them to fully dry.

5. Melt the black candy melts in a plastic bag, snipping off a very small corner to create a piping bag.

6. When the pops are fully set, pipe a horizontal line across the center of the pop and pipe on dots.

Football Helmet Cake Pops •••••••••••••••••

Supplies

- Cake filling of your choice
- Blue candy melts
- Black candy melts
- Blue luster dust
- Red fondant
- White fondant

Tools

- Digital scale
- Sheet pan
- Microwave-safe bowls
- Lollipop sticks
- Plastic bag
- Soft-bristle paintbrush
- 1⅝-inch square-shaped cookie cutter

1. Begin by hand weighing the cake into one-ounce portions. Roll them into balls and set aside on a sheet pan. Place in the fridge while you prepare the candy melts.

2. Melt the blue candy melts according to the directions on the package.

3. Remove the cake from the fridge. Dip each stick into the candy melts and insert them halfway into each cake pop.

4. Once the candy melts have fully set and the cake is back at room temperature, the pops are ready to be dipped. Fully submerge the pops into the blue candy melts and tap off any excess. Allow to set.

5. Once the candy melts have set, lightly dust the entire pop with blue luster dust using the soft-bristle paintbrush.

6. Melt the black candy melts in a small plastic bag and snip off a corner. Pipe the face guard onto the helmet.

7. Roll out the fondant on the thickest setting of the pasta machine and cut out squares with the cookie cutter. Cut the white fondant into ½-inch-wide strips and the red fondant into ¼-inch strips. Glue the strips onto the top of the pop with candy melts and allow to set.

Stadium Cake Pops • • • • • • • • •

Supplies

- Cake filling of your choice
- Green candy melts
- White candy melts
- Gray candy melts
- White and yellow sugar pearls
- Nonpareils

Tools

- Digital scale
- Sheet pan
- Microwave-safe bowls
- Lollipop sticks
- Plastic bags
- Soft-bristle paintbrush
- 1⅝-inch square-shaped cookie cutter

1. Stuff the cookie cutters with the cake mixture, using the palm of your hand to squeeze out any excess cake. Gently push the cake out of each cookie cutter. Chilling your dough ahead of time makes this process easier. Place them on a sheet pan in the refrigerator while you prepare the candy melts.

2. Melt the green and white candy melts according to the directions on the package.

3. Remove the cake from the fridge. Dip each stick into the candy melts and insert them halfway into each cake pop.

4. Once the candy melts have fully set and the cake is back at room temperature, you are ready to dip the pops. Fully submerge the pops into the green candy melts and tap off any excess. Place in a stand and allow to set.

5. Using the soft-bristle paintbrush, dab green candy melts onto the lower half of the pop. While wet, place white and yellow sugar pearls on top and allow to set.

6. Once set, dip the upper half of the pop in the white candy melts and tap off any excess. While still wet, sprinkle nonpareils so that they cover any exposed white candy melts.

7. Melt white and gray candy melts in separate small plastic bags and snip off the corners. With the gray melts, pipe a horizontal line where the green candy melts and nonpareils meet. Using the white candy melts, pipe vertical lines on the field.

Tennis Ball
Cake Pops • • • • • • • • • • • • • •

Supplies

- Cake filling of your choice
- Yellow candy melts
- White candy melts

Tools

- Digital scale
- Sheet pan
- Microwave-safe bowls
- Lollipop sticks
- Plastic bag
- Soft-bristle paintbrush

1. Begin by hand weighing the cake into one-ounce portions. Roll them into balls and flatten the tops until you have flat circles. Place them on a sheet pan in the refrigerator while you prepare the candy melts.

2. Melt the yellow candy melts according to the directions on the package.

3. Remove the cake from the fridge. Dip each stick into the candy melts and insert them halfway into each cake pop.

4. Once the candy melts have fully set and the cake is back at room temperature, you are ready to dip the pops. Fully submerge the pops into the candy melts and tap off any excess. Place in a stand and allow to set.

5. After the pops have set, use a soft-bristle paintbrush to dab on melted candy melts all over the surface to give the pop a textured finish.

6. Melt the white candy melts in a plastic bag and snip off a corner. Pipe on the curved lines and allow to set.